Introductory Note

This volume provides background information on the issues taken up in James P. Cannon's *The Struggle for a Proletarian Party*, and also in Leon Trotsky's *In Defense of Marxism*.

It is divided into four main sections, preceded by an introductory essay originally given as a class in spring 1978 in Morgantown, West Virginia. The first section consists of letters and interviews with Leon Trotsky. These date from June 15, 1937, to June 16, 1939. In the 1937 letters Trotsky supports Cannon's proposal for a decisive fight with the leadership of the Socialist Party over their political support to the popular front government of the Spanish republic. (The Trotskyists favored supporting the republic in the military struggle against Franco's fascist forces, but opposed the bourgeois People's Front government).

Such a fight was certain to lead to a split in the Socialist Party, which the Trotskyists had entered in June 1936, and thus to the reemergence of the Trotskyist movement as an independent political organization.

Trotsky pressed for a new tactical orientation as well. His answer—as well as Cannon's—to the question, "What to do next?" was to turn the Trotskyists sharply toward the trade unions, which were then in great political ferment. Trotskyist forces had been considerably augmented during their stay in the Socialist Party, and Trotsky and Cannon proposed to take advantage of this to build a party that was working class both in program and composition. Trotsky warned of the danger that faced the party if the predominance in sections of the leadership and ranks of middle-class intellectuals and students was unduly prolonged.

Second is a February 1938 letter from James P. Cannon to the International Secretariat of the Movement for the Fourth International (predecessor to the Fourth International founded in September 1938). Cannon describes the results of the founding convention of the Socialist Workers Party, held December 31, 1937–January 3, 1938. This convention decided to devote 90 percent of party activity to the unions.

Third is "The Truth About the Auto Crisis," by George Clarke. This was originally published in March 1940 in the bulletin of the majority faction of the SWP (led by Cannon and supported by Trotsky).

This article describes and evaluates the role of Burnham, Shachtman, and Abern in a dispute that took place in January and February 1939 over policy in the United Auto Workers union. It provides a devastating picture of the leadership methods of the future spearheads of the petty-bourgeois opposition at a time when they had a majority in the SWP Political Committee. It also shows the yawning gap that was appearing between the proletarian and petty-bourgeois sections of the party because of the resistance of the latter to transforming the policy adopted at the founding convention into a reality.

Fourth is a series of six articles by James P. Cannon which appeared in the June 3, June 16, June 20, June 23, June 27, and June 30, 1939, issues of *Socialist Appeal* under the common title of "Toward the Party Convention." These articles were part of a public preconvention discussion of party problems in the *Appeal*.

In these articles Cannon pointed to the need to overcome a degree of stagnation and even the danger of "degeneration" of the party. The danger stemmed, in Cannon's view, from failure to decisively turn toward the unions and break with petty-bourgeois radical circles that were rapidly moving away from Marxism as World War II approached.

The July 1939 convention unanimously reaffirmed the decisions made earlier on work in the trade unions. But the Stalin-Hitler pact, the opening of World War II, and the Soviet invasion of Finland followed soon after. These events brought to the surface the irreconcilable tendencies that had been gestating in the party during the preceding period. The existence of these tendencies had been signaled by the failure of some sections of the party to carry out in deeds the proletarian orientation they had adopted in words. The factional struggle of 1939–40 began.

For a variety of reasons (including the assimilation of the lessons of the 1939–40 struggle by the party), no such crisis afflicts the SWP today as we put into practice our orientation toward the industrial unions.

Nonetheless the items reprinted here contain indispensable lessons for the party today on the importance of timely implementation of such an orientation, the nature of a proletarian party and a proletarian party leadership, and the methods of organizing revolutionary socialist work in the unions.

Fred Feldman

SOME HISTORICAL BACKGROUND TO THE 1939–40 STRUGGLE IN THE SWP

by Fred Feldman

Program is the fundamental determinant of the class nature of any party. A party like the Socialist Workers Party that fights to place the working class in power is a workers' party even if at a given moment a majority of its members are students, lawyers, or Wisconsin dairy farmers.

On the other hand, a party can be predominantly working class in composition and still be capitalist or middle class in its program. A majority of registered Democrats may be workers, but this party is directly controlled by and serves the capitalist ruling class.

A Social Democratic party like the Labour Party in Great Britain serves the ruling class indirectly through the intermediary of the labor bureaucracy and its ideology. Similarly, Stalinist parties like the French Communist Party serve imperialism by way of the Soviet bureaucracy and this is expressed in their basic program.

But composition is far from being irrelevant to program. A party that aims to lead the workers to power needs to be working class in composition. Specifically, it must be centered in the industrial working class, the most powerful section of the class and the section that plays the leading role in decisive battles with the bosses.

If a revolutionary socialist party is predominantly composed of nonworkers, it means that it can't yet make its program a reality. It is not a contender for power. It is still in the initial phase of refining its program and accumulating forces.

The Russian socialists were like that in the first years of the movement. They were mostly students and professional intellectuals arguing for a working-class perspective.

But when the situation changed and workers began to fight, the most determined socialists turned toward that movement. The composition changed rapidly. By 1905 the Bolsheviks were primarily a party of industrial workers, and despite some big downturns they basically remained so.

A radicalization of the working class is a decisive test for a revolutionary party, once it has reached a certain size. If it can't recruit industrial workers and root itself in the industrial working class at such a time, it signifies a contradiction between program and practice that must be resolved. Program or practice must change.

James P. Cannon's *The Struggle for a Proletarian Party* covers a time when this contradiction overtook an important section of the SWP and produced a deep split over basic questions of program, organization, and orientation. The materials in this volume provide some background to Cannon's book.

These items do not center on the theoretical issues that were in dispute, like the nature of the Soviet Union or the necessity of defending the degenerated workers' states against imperialism. They focus instead on the obstacles that the SWP faced in turning toward a radicalized industrial working class.

When the Trotskyists were expelled from the Communist Party for opposing Stalin in 1928, they had few forces and even fewer bases in the unions. These revolutionists devoted themselves to trying to win the most advanced political elements—the members of the Communist Party—to the ideas of the Left Opposition.

At that time they rejected proposals that they devote themselves primarily to "mass work" in the proletariat as a whole, since they had insufficient forces. The class itself was somewhat passive under the impact of the beginning of the depression. These first years until 1933 were a time of great isolation, even though an important nucleus of revolutionists was consolidated around Trotskyist ideas.

After Hitler's rise to power, the International Left Opposition gave up the idea of reforming the parties of the Comintern. Broader arenas opened up as a mass radicalization began to take hold. A centrist group called the American Workers Party came into being, moved toward us, and fused with the Trotskyist organization (the Communist League of America) in 1934.

Then, reflecting a general mass upturn, the Socialist Party turned left, the extreme right wing split away, and a big left wing formed that was more radical than the central leadership around Norman Thomas.

In 1936 the Trotskyists joined the Socialist Party in order to win over this left wing and build a bigger revolutionary organization. They were expelled from the SP a little more than a year later for opposing the SP's political support to the capitalist coalition government during the Spanish civil war. Trotskyists also opposed the SP's endorsement of the Republican candidate for Mayor of New York (La Guardia), who was being supported by the union bureaucrats and the Communist Party.

The Trotskyists took with them the best people in the SP, including virtually the whole Young People's Socialist League. There were now about 2,000 people in the Trotskyist movement.

In the months preceding the founding convention of the SWP Trotsky pressed for a sharp change in orientation. While the Trotskyists had been in the Socialist Party the industrial workers exploded in sitdown strikes and other battles that began the organization of workers in the key industries into the CIO.

The peak of mass activity had passed by the time the Trotskyists formed an independent organization again. But the unions had become areas for sharp debate over political orientation. A new economic crisis developed in 1937, and the approach of the new world war spurred great antiwar sentiment among working people. These developments shook workers' faith in the Roosevelt administration.

The radicalization of workers proved deep and longlasting although it was misled by the Stalinists and the union officialdom. This radicalization did not end definitively until after World War II.

The Trotskyists were not without significant trade union experience. In Minneapolis they had led big Teamsters' strikes and wide-ranging organizing drives. Fractions had been established in the auto and maritime unions, and workers were joining the revolutionary ranks.

Still, less than half the members—and almost none of the newly-won youth—were in industrial unions. And union work had never been the central arena of Trotskyist activity.

On October 10, 1937, Trotsky wrote a letter to James P. Cannon, the central leader of the Trotskyist movement. "The party has only a minority of genuine factory workers," he stated. "This is an inevitable beginning for every revolutionary workers' party. The non-proletarian elements represent a very necessary yeast, and I believe that we can be proud of the good quality of these elements." Nonetheless he pointed to the dangers involved in a composition that was not in line with the party's program and goals.

"The task is naturally not to prevent the influx of intellectuals by artificial methods," he concluded, "but to orient in practice the whole organization toward the factories, the strikes, the unions."

In an October 3, 1937, letter to Cannon he proposed leadership changes to facilitate this: "I have remarked hundreds of times that the worker who remains unnoticed in the 'normal' conditions of party life reveals remarkable qualities in a change of the situation when general formulas and fluent pens are not sufficient, where acquaintance with the life of workers and practical capacities are necessary. . . .

"It is absolutely necessary at the next convention to introduce in the local and central committees as many workers as possible."

In a letter to the International leadership written in February 1938, James P. Cannon pointed out a gap that had opened up between the leadership and the ranks in implementing trade union work while the Trotskyists had been in the SP:

"The locals and branches, on their own initiative, in various localities developed trade union activity, established contact and broadened their experience and connections in this field," he wrote, and concluded: "The necessary transformation from the propaganda circle to mass work is finding its full reflection only belatedly in the leadership itself.

And since the initiative, for a variety of reasons, could not, or at least did not, come through the National Committee, it had to come from below."

The December 1937–January 1938 convention voted to devote 90 percent of party effort to the union movement, and to make this work the top priority for the central party leadership. But this orientation was not fully carried out.

For in fact a division in the leadership and the ranks was slowly taking shape. It was marked initially not by the existence of a contrary line or a clearly defined alternative orientation, but by reluctance, hesitation, and skepticism about taking the next step in building the party.

Four people were generally known to the ranks as central leaders in the party national office and related institutions. One was James P. Cannon, national secretary of the new party. His roots went back to the Industrial Workers of the World and the Socialist Party left wing before the Russian revolution. Then there was Max Shachtman, a veteran revolutionist who helped found the Communist Party in 1919. His specialty was political journalism. And Martin Abern, who, along with Cannon and Shachtman, had been a founder of the Trotskyist movement in the United States. Fourth was James Burnham, a prominent philosophy professor who had joined the party with the American Workers Party in the 1934 fusion. Of these only Cannon threw himself fully into advancing a turn toward the unions.

There were several reasons for this.

One was the obvious difficulties of making a sharp turn from years devoted largely to propaganda work among voluble politicos to work among politically uneducated but radicalizing workers. This meant rethinking every area of party work and big shifts in party members' personal lives. The weight of this factor should not be exaggerated, however. After all, the years of propaganda work in politicized circles had been aimed precisely at preparing such a shift.

More important was the changing political moods among middle-class intellectuals, journalists, students, and similar types who had been attracted for a time to revolutionary politics. These forces tend to be drawn to whichever of the two decisive contending classes seems the most dynamic and capable of ordering society. The capitalist social crisis shook them loose from their bourgeois moorings and turned them toward the left, but the crisis had dragged on and the workers—especially on a world scale—could hardly be said to be scoring tremendous victories.

Hitler had triumphed in Germany; Franco was heading for power in Spain; a workers' upsurge was successfully derailed by Stalinist class collaboration; Czechoslovakia and Austria came under Nazi rule; Stalin was killing off all of Lenin's associates and murdering millions of other people in the purges; World War II was approaching and there seemed to be no force on earth that could stop it; and the Fourth International, the only fully conscious revolutionary force, remained tiny.

True, the rise of the CIO in the United States had been a historic victory for labor, but the CIO bureaucrats were successfully guiding the movement into the Roosevelt camp, and fascist formations in the U.S. had begun to grow at a more rapid clip.

Pessimism and demoralization spread like an epidemic in middle-class circles. Their professions and middle-class prospects preserved them from the conditions that forced workers to fight, and made it easier for them to adapt to the dominant bourgeoisie; and their lack of ties to the mass workers' movement deprived them of any sense of its tremendous power. The middle-class radicals—typified by people like Max Eastman—began to move rightward and their influence was strongly felt in the party. Many party leaders like Shachtman and Burnham had worked closely with this milieu, and Burnham had basically always belonged to it.

For them the pressure to turn the party's face in another direction was pressure to devote themselves wholly to building a proletarian party and to break with old, comfortable milieus. It meant looking at their activities and plans in the first place from that point of view. But many had gnawing doubts about the real possibilities of building a revolutionary working-class movement.

In *The Struggle for a Proletarian Party*, Cannon describes a classic statement of this mood, recording a conversation with Burnham about taking a full-time party assignment:

"I proposed concretely that he end the two-for-a-nickel business of instructing college students who have no intention of connecting themselves with the labor movement, and devote his energies and talents entirely to the party [in the capacity of national secretary]. After 'thinking it over' for a day or so he rejected the proposal. The reason he gave was somewhat astounding: he said he was not fully convinced of the wisdom of devoting himself to a cause which might not be victorious in his lifetime! Naturally, I could not give him any guarantees."

Burnham was a central party leader with considerable prestige. Imagine the effect his attitude had on younger, less experienced members who were considering whether to commit themselves fully.

The youth movement of that day also presented a problem. The YPSL was very different from today's YSA. The great majority of its members had come from the loose and clique-ridden Social Democracy and Social-Democratic ideas still influenced them. Interestingly, much of their work was also tinged with ultraleftism, for instance in the struggle against fascism. They had few youth of working-class origin and almost none from the oppressed nationalities. Still they were good material. Trotsky summed up the problem in a May 27, 1939, letter:

"I continue to be of the opinion that you have *too many petty-bourgeois boys and girls* who are very good and devoted to the party, but who do not fully realize that their duty is not to discuss among themselves, but to penetrate into the fresh milieu of workers." [*In Defense of Marxism*, (New York: Pathfinder, 1942, 1955), p. 201 (2018 printing)].

A fourth and particularly damaging problem was the Abern clique. This was a grouping around Martin Abern, who had taken a strong dislike to Cannon. The reasons for this are unclear. In any case, he devoted his political activity to organizing against Cannon.

He organized a grouping of people who had one or another grievance against the leadership. In a small, isolated movement under a lot of pressure in a capitalist society, there were always plenty of irritations for Abern to feed on.

Abern and his following formed a kind of mutual admiration, advancement, and protection association. They sought to push each other forward and to snipe at Cannon or at people who accepted Cannon's leadership. They subordinated political considerations to this.

One method used by this grouping was the secret circulation of material and information about what was going on in the political committee and in different branches. It was inevitably one-sided information. This kind of rumor-mongering gave the participants in Abern's group the feeling of being in the know. It made it possible for Abern to line people up on political questions or organizational disputes without another side being presented. It poisoned the atmosphere, and undermined the ability of leading bodies to discuss freely and function effectively.

The Abern clique represented the opposite of revolutionary Marxist politics—with them, subjective criteria and considerations of prestige or revenge ranked higher than objective political needs. This wasn't entirely deliberate. They were just blinded by hatred of Cannon and admiration for each other.

The Abern grouping was a product of the movement's isolated and somewhat ingrown existence over many years. It was an obstacle to a turn toward the working class. The group's politics, in so far as it had any, were conservative. It had opposed every major turn made by the party in the past—after all Cannon was for it! Thus it took a negative stance toward the fusion with the American Workers Party and the entry into the Socialist Party. It was in the nature of the group that its eyes were always turned inward. They didn't look outward to the unions, because they were primarily concerned about the impact of any change on their own position. And they naturally latched on to any signs of discontent caused by new moves and developments. On top of this, they tended to regard the trade unions as Cannon's "turf."

Now this kind of grouping had a certain appeal to those who had developed in the loose, undisciplined talk-shop atmosphere of the Socialist Party. And many of the Abernites were people of real organizational and literary talent. They emerged as the leaders of the youth movement, which they tried to use as a base against the party leadership. Under the given historical circumstances, this tended to cut off the political development of the bulk of the youth. Abern built up his group by catering to their errors, fears, prejudices, and hesitations. They were reinforced in the tendency to subordinate basic political considerations to organizational and personal concerns.

A majority of the Political Committee was made up of supporters of Abern plus Burnham and Shachtman. The problem was not that so many students and intellectuals had joined the party. That was positive. The problem was that a key part of the leadership adapted to this layer instead of educating it and integrating it into a proletarian party—and this section also adapted to middle-class layers outside the movement who were heading rightward politically.

While Cannon and others tried to press forward the turn, little fundamental progress was made. Moods of discontent spread in the party, which seemed to be stagnating. In effect, no new orientation had been put into practice to replace the orientation toward the Socialist Party.

One result of the long delay in carrying out the turn—which resulted in missing some good party-building opportunities—was growing tension between party unionists and the nonworker elements, and between the unionists and a big section of the national leadership. They were moving in opposite directions.

The problems were further complicated by the weight of supporters of Burnham, Shachtman, and Abern on the Political Committee. They often had a majority.

These problems reached explosive proportions in what became known as the "auto crisis" of January 1939, which was vividly described in an article written by George Clarke for the majority faction in the 1939–40 struggle.

A split was developing in the United Auto Workers at the time between an open right wing led by Homer Martin and a group of bureaucrats including the Stalinists. Rival conventions were called: Martin's for Detroit, the Stalinist-backed one for Cleveland.

Neither group represented a left wing. Both were led by self-seeking bureaucrats. But a tactical decision had to be made.

The leaders of the auto union fraction met and adopted a policy. Auto workers would form a third group calling for keeping the union united and opposing both bureaucratic factions. The auto fraction met and voted unanimously for this.

The Political Committee in New York voted to reject this policy. Cannon was in Europe at the time. The PC ordered the publication of an editorial by Burnham in the *Appeal* basically endorsing the right-wing Martin group's convention. An issue of the *Appeal* was published carrying this line.

As George Clarke wrote, "Observe here . . . that there was no motion, no suggestion, no intimation that before adopting a policy completely at loggerheads with the Field Committee and the National Auto Conference, the committee was in the slightest degree interested in gaining additional information from the comrades on the scene. Not even a hint that some PC comrade or the entire PC might go out to the field to get information and debate the policy; not even a hint that one of the field comrades might be called into New York for the same purpose." Without talking to a single auto worker or trade unionist, Burnham just sat down at his typewriter and tapped out a policy.

What was involved here was an entirely tactical decision, based on a conjunctural estimate of two rival factions in the UAW. Even if the PC felt obliged to reverse a local tactical decision on principled grounds, it was totally unprecedented and wrong to do so without thorough consultation with the members who were to carry the decision out.

The Martin group now announced it was quitting the CIO, the industrial union movement the party was committed to building. This decisive shift to the right by Martin was sure to isolate him further, and the auto fraction leaders now decided that SWP supporters in Auto should attend the Cleveland convention of the anti-Martin group.

But Burnham was able to carry his position by a 3–2 plurality, along with a motion demanding instant obedience. Burnham and Abern threatened to resign if the motion wasn't carried out.

Opposition throughout the party grew and Burnham finally had to cave in, assenting to a change in the tactic along lines favored by the fraction. He then sent out a letter denouncing the fraction. He had yielded, he wrote, because "the attempt to carry out the policy of the P.C. majority (that is, the policy of the party) would be certain to lead to a major internal party crisis." Burnham's attempt to transform three people into the party didn't hide the fact that the cause of the problem was that there was no support in the ranks or the National Committee for Burnham's policy.

The fact that Burnham's proposal was wrong

was of minor importance. Errors are inevitable when inexperienced people start trying to find their way in doing party work in the unions.

The whole incident was a model of how not to do union work and how a leadership can discredit itself in the eyes of the party ranks.

In a subsequent meeting of the Political Committee, Burnham and Abern were said to have complained, "It isn't so much that the Field comrades opposed us" but that "this dispute would never have arisen if Cannon were here. They would never have dared challenge Cannon the way they did us."

Clarke comments: "Is it possible to convince such people by a citation from the record that Cannon always seeks out complete information before jumping to a policy, especially on trade union matters; that where there is disagreement on a practical matter where no political principle is involved between himself and the field comrades, he first of all attempts to persuade them that he is correct; that failing to persuade them—even though firmly convinced of the justice of his position—he yields in their favor? Can you explain to these people that this is an essential quality of proletarian organization."

An example of Cannon's practice is provided by Farrell Dobbs in *Teamster Power.* In the chapter "Tobin Backs Down" Dobbs recounts a discussion of a tactical issue concerning the reinstatement of Minneapolis Teamsters Local 574 into the Teamsters Union.

At that time, Cannon (who was asked by the fraction to come to Minneapolis for consultation) strongly disagreed with the decision taken by the fraction.

Dobbs says, "We explained why we thought the proposed settlement with [Teamsters president] Tobin should be accepted. Jim, in turn, informed us of the hesitations among the national Trotskyist leaders about taking such a course. As the discussion then unfolded the Teamster comrades were unanimous in expressing confidence that we could retain decisive leadership control in the proposed new local. We also argued strongly for party approval of our recommendation."

Dobbs continues: "There was no question of principle involved. It was simply a matter of a choice in tactics. So he [Cannon] agreed that the party should give us the benefit of the doubt on the tactical decision. . . ."

"I don't fully agree with the decision," Jim told us, in effect, "but I will take full responsibility with you, even if it goes bad."

Burnham and Abern made the fatal mistake of thinking that party members can be led primarily by resort to formal authority. They looked at the party constitution and saw right there in black and white that the Political Committee is empowered to make decisions between meetings of the National Committee. So they started to bark out commands without regard to reality, their own experience in the given area of work, or the opinions of others who were more experienced. And Shachtman, who wavered on the concrete policy, went along with Burnham and Abern on the propriety of this procedure. This reflected his vacillating drift into the petty-bourgeois camp.

The whole system of democratic centralism assumes that the leadership will be alert to the thinking and judgments of the ranks; and even more that the leadership will submit to the test of events and change a policy that proves unrealistic.

The whole incident demonstrated a professorial, thoroughly petty-bourgeois refusal to collaborate with and learn from the working-class forces in the field. They thought the status of leaders and official titles put them beyond all that—just like bureaucrats.

The fact is that while a combat party like the SWP operates on the basis of firm centralism, it is primarily teamwork and collaboration that counts in the making of day-to-day decisions. Political leadership authority comes from the ability to contribute to and guide this process.

Burnham and Abern had forgotten Trotsky's good advice: "A functionary of a revolutionary party should have in the first place a good ear, and only in the second place a good tongue." A party leadership that remembers this stores up tremendous moral authority with the members, which can be brought to bear when decisive and disciplined action with a minimum of discussion is needed.

By the summer of 1939 Cannon had become alarmed at the problems the party was having. In a series of articles that were part of a public discussion preceding the July 1939 convention he noted a degree of "stagnation" in the party, and referred to the existence of "formal agreement" among the leadership about turning to the unions. Citing the desertion of the radical movement by intellectual figures, he stated:

"Our convention must let the dead bury the dead and turn the face of the party to the workers, who are the real source of power and of inspiration and of well-grounded optimism."

And: "Our sluggishness in making the abrupt turn to mass work with all force and energy; the persistence of old habits of our days of isolation as a propaganda circle; our failure to reach new, fresh strata of workers; our hesitation, half-hearted, at the brink of the great stream of the workers' mass movement—herein is the root of all our evils."

In the ranks of the party, anger and frustration were building up. Contributions to the preconvention discussion showed a groping for some way to get the party off dead center. The Ohio and Michigan district committee, a strong base of the party's trade union orientation, wrote protesting the slackness that they saw around them:

"From the ranks the party must now exact the highest discipline, responsibility and activity. We cannot tolerate laxness in dues payments, neglect of assignments, tardiness and absence, disorderly conduct at party functions and affairs. Above all, we cannot tolerate further the notion of first and second-class citizenship: those who can do the work and take the risks and those who exempt themselves for innumerable personal reasons from 'sticking their necks out.' We are determined to be a party of action. He who shuns such action signifies his desire to be out of the party."

It was clear that a sharp turn was called for, but before this could be carried out the internal situation exploded. When the Soviet Union invaded Finland in August 1939, following the Stalin-Hitler pact, a wave of anti-Soviet propaganda engulfed the country. Shachtman, Burnham, and virtually the entire middle-class membership of the party were swept away by it, refusing to defend the Soviet Union in a conflict with imperialism. While rejecting defense of the Soviet Union in wartime, they went on a war footing against the party and eventually split.

In the end the minority challenged the whole program of the party and its democratic-centralist structure. Trotsky called them the petty-bourgeois opposition, not only because of their class composition—which wasn't at all accidental, of course—but because of their program, which wavered between the capitalists and the workers in search of a mythical "third camp"; and because of their orientation, which reflected a preference for cultivated discussion among intellectual skeptics to building a party of workers.

The root of the 1939 conflict was the approaching war and the political shifts and pressures that grew as it approached. But a crisis of orientation in the leadership was a central component of the crisis. A section of the leadership resisted taking a further step toward making our program a reality through turning the party toward the industrial unions. They resisted transforming the SWP into a party made up in its majority of industrial workers, at a time when it was objectively possible to accomplish this.

Carried past a certain point which could not be predicted in advance, this resistance inevitably fostered a challenge to our program, which points to the workers as the revolutionary class and calls for building a revolutionary party based in the most powerful sectors of that class.

Today we are carrying out a major turn toward the industrial workers after a long period when party work focused on struggles occurring outside the unions. There are many reasons why we face a much more favorable situation today in making this turn. Some important ones, in my opinion, are:

1. We have launched our turn in a timely way when the radicalization of labor is in its early stages;

2. U.S. imperialism and Stalinism were actually headed toward the peaks of their power when the SWP began its turn in the late 1930s. And the labor bureaucracy was beginning to consolidate its grip on the new CIO unions in the wake of the initial upsurge. Today all of these counterrevolutionary forces are in decline.

The changes in the world situation can be typified by comparing the impact of the Spanish civil war on radicals and working-class fighters with that of the Vietnamese struggle, which played a similar role in many respects for our generation.

The bloody betrayal of the Spanish workers by Stalin and their ultimate defeat at the hands of the

Francoists was a deep blow to the morale of the working-class movement, and even more to the morale of its middle-class periphery. In Vietnam, despite the betrayal by Moscow and Peking, the rebel forces emerged victorious.

These changed world conditions mean that the morale problems on the scale of those that confronted the party in the late 1930s do not confront us today.

3. The party leadership in the center and in the branches is united in driving forward the turn.

4. The YSA is very different from the YPSL. It fully supports the turn, and its work in building a revolutionary student organization is an important part of strengthening the party in the turn. And the YSA has been educated in our proletarian traditions, and not in a Social Democratic tradition as were most members of the YPSL.

5. We have at our disposal and have assimilated into our structure and tradition the lessons of the 1940 fight.

Of course if we were to falter and not do what needs to be done, as happened in the 1930s, similar problems in a different form would eventually occur. But that is not the direction the party is headed in.

LETTERS FROM LEON TROTSKY

THE SITUATION IN THE SP AND OUR NEXT TASKS

June 15, 1937

Dear Comrades:

I have received a copy of Cannon's letter of June 9 to Joe [Carter] on the situation in the SP and our next tasks. As far as I can judge from here, I find the letter excellent in every respect. It would be fatal to lose time waiting for a new, more favorable "situation." If we remain passive, time from now on will work against us. The situation has become so clear and concentrated that we can even establish a five-month plan.

A. During this summer the Spanish civil war must come to a denouement. The fight on this issue within the proletarian vanguard cannot but become more acute.

B. The persecutions and executions in the USSR are developing at such a feverish tempo that in the next months we can expect a transformation of quantity into quality. In any case, before the twentieth anniversary of the October revolution, the Stalinist regime will stand revealed before the workers to an incomparably greater extent than it is today.

C. The Blum experiment seems to be approaching its natural end, that is, bankruptcy. The policy of the People's Front will receive a mortal blow.

D. The full Commission of Inquiry will hold its final sessions in September. We can have no doubts about its conclusions, which must and will be annihilating for the Stalinist clique and for the Comintern bureaucracy.

The coincidence of all these factors promises to open an extremely favorable situation for our activity during the coming fall. It would be criminal to meet this new situation as prisoners of Thomas, Trager, Tyler, and Company. No, we must again appear on the scene as an independent party. It seems to me here that the anniversary of the October revolution is the deadline for the establishment of our complete political independence.

This plan demands a vigorous mobilization of our cadres for a new strategic line. This is impossible without a weekly. The question of reestablishing our own weekly is a hundred times more important than all the statutory considerations and diplomatic prudence. Our attack against the right-wingers as the agents of the Stalinist-reformist hangmen of the Russian revolution as well as the Spanish revolution must be so vigorous and relentless that the petty bureaucrats will have to forget the purely formal and organizational questions. We cannot discuss with Altmanites and the Wisconsin people as with comrades. We must denounce them as traitors and rascals. Events will justify our tone in the eyes of the rank and filers. Only by such an attack can we prevent hesitations among our sympathizers and the best elements of the Clarity faction. In this respect I entirely agree, as I said before, with Cannon's letter. As far as I can judge, on the basis of written reports and conversations with some American comrades, the coming turn can be accomplished without frictions in our own ranks, under the condition that the National Committee gives the comrades clear, precise, and courageous directives.

Permit me to concretize the five-month plan hypothetically:

By July 15 our comrades must be mobilized for the radical turn.

The first issue of our weekly must appear in the second half of July.

August and September: our campaign against the right wing and, in the second place, against the centrists.

During October we must reestablish entirely our organizational apparatus.

Not later than November 7 we must appear as an independent party.

Since we are preparing to step beyond the remnants of the SP, we must simultaneously begin more systematic and persistent work within the CP. This party cannot possibly be left intact by the above-mentioned political factors. Crises and splits are inevitable. It is possible that by fall we can prepare an amalgamation of a part of the CP with our own independent organization.

I do not speak here about our work in the trade unions, especially in the CIO. That, generally speaking, is the most important task before us. However, this task too demands our independence as a condition for free and courageous activity in strikes and in the unions.

Fraternally,
Wolfe [Trotsky]

MORE PEDAGOGICAL PATIENCE TOWARD NEW ELEMENTS

September 11, 1937

Dear Comrade Cannon:

1. I don't believe that personal correspondence with Sneevliet could, in the *present* situation, change anything. Sneevliet is very stubborn. He broke organizational relations with the International Secretariat; he is very hostile to the Americans, who "betrayed" the Fourth International. He is embittered by the permanent misfortunes of his policy in Holland. He puts more stock in the small bureau of the NAS than in his international connections. He latched onto the POUM in the hope of having a counterweight to our tendency, and the terrible collapse of the POUM embittered him even more. He is totally unapproachable today. After your national convention, if it is successful—and I am sure it will be—you will have more possibility to influence him.

2. That the Brandlerites and Lovestoneites have entered the Noah's ark of the London Bureau is very favorable: it will only augment the centrifugal tendencies of this famous "revolutionary unity." I don't know if the Lovestoneites have any intelligent people, possibly, but their tendency is fundamentally stupid. In the Oehlerites you find at least some geometric construction—useless but curious. The writings of the Lovestoneites are only profoundly boring.

3. From conversations with visitors (and they are numerous) I am under the impression that we are in complete isolation from the Stalinist party. That's very, very regrettable. The closest obstacle is the Stalinists. Systematic work should be begun immediately. Even a small, modest subcommittee for that purpose could prepare the ground for the larger penetration in this milieu.

4. Our organization will become attractive to very different people in the next period, and not only for the best of them. Public life in the States is very agitated, and the recent announcement of the new crisis will aggravate the disquietude, the fighting spirit, and . . . the confusion. We can't avoid having this confusion in our ranks. Our comrades are "too" educated, "too" accustomed to precise, elaborated conceptions and slogans. They have a contempt for everybody who is not ideologically "O.K." It is very dangerous. A developing and alive party must represent—to a certain extent—the different tendencies, disquietudes and, I repeat, even the confusion in the vanguard of the working class. Too much confusion is, of course, not good but a sound proportion can be established only through practice. More pedagogical patience is absolutely necessary on the part of our comrades toward the new and fresh elements. That is the genuine meaning of party "democracy." I believe that for the next period the emphasis must be put on the *democracy*, not on the *centralism*. The necessary equilibrium between them will be established on the basis of the new experience.

As I see from a short remark in your letter, you plan to come to Mexico. It is not necessary to say that Natalia and I would be very glad to have you again in our home.

With best greetings,
Leon Trotsky

FOR A REGIME OF GENUINE DEMOCRACY

September 11, 1937

Dear Comrade Glotzer:

The Despres left yesterday for Chicago. We spent some very agreeable days together in Taxco.

Before them we had a visit from the Heisler family. We discussed in a very friendly manner the present situation in the Socialist Party, etc. I am very interested to know if the differences with Heisler are now resolved.

The creation of an independent party with about two thousand members is a very important step forward. The inner regime in the party is of the greatest importance. It must be a regime of genuine democracy. I agree with you on the matter totally. Democracy presupposes not only a formal political but a pedagogical approach, to new members and to every workers' audience. It is correct that the leadership should be patient in its approach to the membership as the party should be in its approach to the working masses. That far I agree with you. But there are methods of fighting for party democracy which are very dangerous to this aim. The present leadership—I mean all its members—is not an accidental one: it is a result of a selection, of a long period of struggle. In three to five years, new experiences can induce important changes in the composition and in the mentality of the leadership. But trying to change the leadership by some too-impatient, too-sharp measures can be fatal, and I can't conceal my impression that there are some disquieting symptoms in your letter. Possibly my impression is false; all the better.

In an old and warm friendship,
L. Trotsky

MORE THOUGHTS ON THE PARTY REGIME

October 3, 1937

Dear Comrade Cannon:

Yesterday I sent you a letter concerning some important matters, but it is necessary to write you again today.

1. I read a moment ago a letter from Harry Milton to Rae [Spiegel]. I have read some of his letters from Spain, and I heard yesterday from Rae that he made a very good speech on Spain before a large meeting and that everybody was astonished at his success, himself more than anybody. Finally, he mentioned that the National Committee had decided to send him on a tour alone and not with Comrade Goldman, as had been scheduled. This fact seems extremely important and symptomatic. I observed another worker from your organization here, Comrade Lankin. In the presence of [Jack] Weber, F., and other comrades, he remained very silent, but worked all the time. Then he remained for a longer time with us. He revealed a great deal of life and fighting experience, of psychological observation and political considerations of great value. Such comrades are necessary in our party committees, in the central committee as well as in the local committees. I have remarked hundreds of times that the worker who remains unnoticed in the "normal" conditions of party life reveals remarkable qualities in a change of the situation when general formulas and fluent pens are not sufficient, where acquaintance with the life of workers and practical capacities are necessary. Under such conditions a gifted worker reveals a sureness of himself and reveals also his general political capabilities.

Predominance in the organization of intellectuals is inevitable in the first period of the development of the organization. It is at the same time a big handicap to the political education of the more gifted workers. All this is a very elementary truth known to you, naturally, for many years. But what is the practical question? I talked about the question with Comrade Weber. It is absolutely necessary at the next convention to introduce in the local and central committees as many workers as possible. To a worker, activity in the leading party body is at the same time a higher political school. Some of the new worker members of the party committees will show then that they are not sufficiently fit for the post: they can be replaced at the next convention. A selection of the most capable, devoted elements for the leading bodies can proceed only slowly and naturally is never finished. A certain risk in the placing of these new comrades is inevitable. If only a third of the new worker members in the local and central committees reveal themselves as fit, the result is excellent.

The difficulty is that in every organization there are traditional committee members and that different secondary, factional, and personal considerations play too great a role in the composition of the list of candidates. The task is to break with routine, which is the beginning of bureaucratism; to convince the organization and especially its leading stratum (which is more difficult) of the necessity of a systematic renewal of the composition of all the leading bodies of the party. Naturally, the renewal can never be complete; a nucleus selected by the whole experience of the past is necessary in order to preserve the continuity of the party's politics.

2. The development of these considerations seems to me of some importance also from the viewpoint of *party democracy*. This aspect cannot be overestimated. What is party democracy?

a. The strictest observance of the party statutes by the leading bodies (regular conventions, necessary period of discussion, right of the minority to express its opinions in the party meetings and in the press).

b. A patient, friendly, to a certain point pedagogical attitude on the part of the central committee and its members toward the rank and file, including the objectors and the discontented, because it is not a great merit to be satisfied "with anybody who is satisfied with me." When Lenin asked for the expulsion of Ordzhonikidze from the party (1923), he said very correctly that the discontented party member has the right to be turbulent, but not a member of the central committee. Methods of psychological "terrorism," including a haughty or sarcastic manner of answering or treating every objection, criticism, or doubt—it is, namely, this journalistic or "intellectualistic" manner which is insufferable to workers and condemns them to silence.

c. The solely formal object of the democratic rules as indicated under (a) and the solely negative measures—not to terrorize, not to ridicule—under (b) are not sufficient. The central committee as well as every local committee must be in permanent, active, and informal contact with the rank and file, especially when a new slogan or a new campaign is in preparation or when it is necessary to verify the results of an accomplished campaign. Not every member of the central committee is capable of such an informal contact, and not every member has the time for this or the occasion, which depends not only upon goodwill and a particular psychology but also upon the profession and the corresponding milieu. In the composition of the central committee it is necessary to have not only good organizers and good speakers, writers, administrators, but also people closely connected with the rank and file, organically representative of them.

3. During the last few weeks I received several letters from Comrades Glotzer and Abern, written to the effect that they don't wish to have any special group, in view of the absence of principled differences, and that they are willing to cooperate in the most loyal and sincere manner, but that in the party regime there are psychological remnants of a Versailles treaty imposed by the former majority upon the former minority (second-class party and committee members and so on). From the other side, I heard from Comrade Weber that his personal attempts to reestablish comradely relationships with the former minority did not succeed.

Don't you believe that some concrete and sincere step could be made by the leaders of the former majority in order to eliminate the psychological remnants of the old struggle? What could this step be? In the first place, an open discussion in the committee with the most representative comrades of the former minority: Have we any principled difference with you? What are your organizational, or practical, or personal objections? Now, at the beginning of a great new chapter in the life of the party, we on our own part are absolutely ready to eliminate all the hindrances to close and harmonious cooperation. We are ready, for example, to eliminate anything resembling a factional caucus in the central committee. You find that the party regime is not sufficiently democratic? We are absolutely ready to accept every practical suggestion in order to eliminate any bureaucratic tendency and amplify the general party democracy, and so on. Such a discussion should be conducted without official procedure; that is, without concern for formulation in the minutes, etc. If the first discussion of such kind reveals itself as more or less promising, it could be repeated during the convention, especially with the consent of the members of the new National Committee.

The initiative should issue from the "majority," which only by general goodwill can disarm the minority. Let us imagine that some of the minority representatives, in spite of the best will on your part, continue their factional position. But the question is: Who will win by such a march of events? Not the factionalists surely. They will isolate themselves from their own closest friends. For the inner education and cohesion of the central committee, such a sincere attempt to reestablish the full mutual confidence could have only the best influence.

My letter of yesterday, like this one, is written in view of the coming party discussion and the convention. Yesterday I tried tentatively to suggest a political "general line" for the next period of party activity. The present letter considers especially the inner regime. I am a bit embarrassed by my too abstract approach to the concrete questions now before you. Some things in my letters can appear to you only as vague generalities without any application—but there is nothing to be done. In spite of the visits and the airmail I remain only an observer from afar. You and the other comrades will see for yourselves what of these suggestions can be of use and what cannot.

My best regards and wishes,
Hansen [Trotsky]

P.S.—Some comrades continue to characterize Stalinism as "bureaucratic centrism." This characterization is now totally out of date. On the international arena Stalinism is no longer centrism, but the crudest form of opportunism and social patriotism. See Spain!

RESULTS OF THE ENTRY AND THE NEXT TASKS

October 6, 1937

TROTSKY: I believe it would be impermissible to devote an important part of the convention to discussion of this question. The question itself is now resolved by the march of events, by developments. On the other hand, I believe it would be impossible to totally avoid the question of opinion on this question. But there should be just two short declarations, because the NC in its report is obliged to mention the fact of entry into the SP: "We remained a year, we entered with such and such forces, and after a year we have drawn the following balance sheet. We can judge our entry as a success. I personally believed the SP was stronger than it was in reality: I believed it had 20,000 members, but it was weaker. I believe we committed some tactical mistakes during our sojourn: we made some unnecessary concessions, such as giving up the *Socialist Appeal* and the practical mistake of giving up the printing press, possibly connected with a long-term perspective, but on the whole we gained so and so." Were I of the majority, I would say that. "Still, I would repeat this experience and I believe the excellent comrades from the minority were wrong and I right." If anybody asked me, "Do you not believe that as an independent party we would have had more success?" I would say, "My dear friend, it was possible to discuss this question before but now we know by international comparison that that is not so." The CPs were growing, the People's Fronts were established, the SPs began to split more or less. I don't see why our tendency would have been successful only in the U.S. when in Holland, Belgium, and France, where we had independent sections, we did not grow.

M: What about Indochina?

TROTSKY: I cannot say, as I know very little about Indochina.

M: Our French section says Indochina is the best section and grew.

TROTSKY: But in Indochina there is no big CP and no SP; thus they are before the working class as the only working-class independent party.

M: But that shows there were other factors in each country to account for the growth or lack of growth of our section.

TROTSKY: I know the reasons for our sections remaining stagnant: the "prosperity" created conditions for People's Fronts in the different countries, and then there were the Moscow trials. Even people who had doubts, who had aversions, even workers, also had doubts about our section. The fact that in the U.S. we were in the SP and connected with the left wing, in daily work, convinced them that we could not have connections with the fascists. That was a factor not foreseen by anybody, of course, but it helped. To deny that means only to have factional pride and stubbornness. That it was unforeseen we can agree. Now it is absolutely clear that the American section is the only one that had important successes. It was covered by the raincoat of the SP, and Thomas was a member of the Committee for Defense, and we could get Dewey and the others. It was a very happy experience. What you won is not from the Hippodrome meeting but from the SP, and perhaps also from the Hippodrome for the SP, and from there for the "Trotskyites."

You say you couldn't win people because you were enclosed in the SP. But in such a case why didn't the Oehlerites, or other groups who were independent, win them? They had a bad policy? But the POUM had a bad policy, but since it was the only left group its membership jumped from 8,000 to 40–50,000 in two weeks. Don't think that these alleged revolutionary elements are so educated in advance that they said, "Yes, Oehler is independent but wrong," or "Weisbord is not such a good Marxist."

Does that mean that I would enter another party? Yes, if I could enter the CP as a party of the Fourth International, I would enter today.

M: Given the conditions as they are, are we then doomed to stagnation?

TROTSKY: That's possible. That is not excluded. I believe during some months or a year we will not double our membership, we may even remain stagnant—like water before boiling, it becomes warmer and warmer.

Secondly, the reasons are different, but they can be reduced to a general reason: that the organization as an organization is young, was developing under extremely difficult conditions, has too great a number of nonproletarian elements with their individualistic minds; the experience of a small group doesn't give the leaders the possibility to win the confidence of the members because only the events, the developments, can confirm the correctness of the line of the leadership and affirm its authority. For my part, I believe that the authority of the leadership is more important than before. The members will realize that the leadership, in spite of secondary errors, showed firmness and a capacity for activity and were incomparably superior to the leaders of the SP, not only in matters of propaganda but in conditions based on the political activity of the party.

Naturally, the party must allow considerable latitude to its leaders. But on the other hand, it is impossible to have credit with the organization if the authority of the leadership is not confirmed by experience itself, by a good policy, and by success. It is necessary to accumulate this capital, and only then will the leadership have the necessary latitude in action. To win this authority it is necessary to have a good policy.

It would be fantastic to ask from the leadership that they commit no errors. What we ask is to correct errors in time, so that the errors don't become fatal.

If the dissolution of the caucus and the abandonment of the paper had continued for a long time, it would have meant the death of our tendency. It retreated to win a breathing spell, and when it realized that there was nothing to be gained and everything to be lost it corrected its error. I consider it an error but it can only be considered as a test of the strength of the offensive, of the plans of the leaders. And a leadership which corrects its errors in time is a good leadership.

It is absolutely necessary to have the confidence of the rank and file. I mentioned the most important condition of this confidence—a good policy. The policy must be prepared with the understanding of the rank and file. It occurs often that the leadership, which sees a situation very well and has a very correct decision, imposes on the organization some imperative action, pushed by impatience, because the leadership feels that if we now begin a discussion of one or two months, we will lose precious time. It may be a correct idea, but by gaining here a month I may lose a year, because the rank and file regards this change and speed with astonishment; and if success of the policy should be lacking, then the rank and file says, "The leadership was wrong; it bears the responsibility." And thus I lose a year to repair the results of my impatience.

That's why it is important, especially for a young organization, not to be impatient and to prepare for every new decision. First of all it is important to observe very strictly the statutes of the organization—regular meetings of the rank and file, discussions before conventions, regular conventions and the right of the minority to express its opinion (there should be a comradely attitude and no threats of expulsion). You know that was never, *never* done in the old [Russian] party. Expulsion of a comrade was a tragic event, and was done only for moral reasons and not because of a critical attitude. We had some comrades in opposition after the revolution. We had comrades who became specialists in criticism, not in principled matters but in minor ones. There was Stukhov, an intelligent man and a courageous one, as well as witty, and at every party meeting he found something to say, prefacing with a joke, and he had applause. Imagine during the civil war—there were many things to object to the leadership, and he took advantage of it. But nobody proposed to expel him, but from time to time we explained to the members, and he began to lose his audience, and after a while Stukhov became a ridiculous figure.

He was one from the top of the party. In every body there were such Stukhovs. It was not a question of Stukhov but of the education of the party membership, an education that rejects unhealthy criticism, opposition only for the sake of opposition. I believe it is absolutely necessary also for the leadership to be very patient, to listen very attentively, very reasonably to criticism. But the most important thing is to change the social composition of the organization—make it a workers' organization. A worker comes to the meeting; he knows everything is imperfect; his pay is imperfect, his conditions of work are imperfect, his life is imperfect; he is consequently more patient, more realistic. When you have a meeting of 100 people and between them 60–70–80 are workers, then the 20 intellectuals, petty bourgeois, become ten times more cautious on the question of criticism. It's a more serious, more firm audience. But when there are 100 intellectuals, everybody has something to say. Party life is just a period of discussion. That's why the social composition is the most important thing, but it cannot be done artificially. If you have a party of 20,000 workers, the unemployed are also workers; but in a party of 1,000, the unemployed only aggravate the situation.

THE SOCIAL COMPOSITION OF THE PARTY

October 10, 1937

Dear Comrade Cannon:

I fear that the fragmentary character of my previous letters may lead to misunderstanding. I insist upon the fact that the general line of development of the Fourth International will be connected in the next period with a new crisis and the inevitable disintegration of People's Front policies and the Third International. This perspective seems to me very important for the general orientation. I heard that some comrades are more or less, if not pessimistic, at least reconciled to the idea that the growth of our organization will be very difficult and slow. The perspective of a sharp turn which can open the greatest possibilities for us is thus necessary not only for a clear orientation but also for moral encouragement.

However, the above-indicated perspective is too general. We don't know precisely when the crisis will begin, with what tempo and to what depth in its first phase it will influence the working class movement and its political organizations. Possibly, even probably, the next year will be a transitory period before going into the "great turn." Such a possibility should be indicated in the basic document [for the coming convention] in order to prevent confusion and disillusionment.

But whether the development in the next period is slower or quicker, one question retains its tremendous importance for us: that of the social composition of the party. It must be considered with the utmost attention.

The party has only a minority of genuine factory workers. This is an inevitable beginning for every revolutionary workers' party everywhere, and especially in the United States. The nonproletarian elements represent a very necessary yeast, and I believe that we can be proud of the good quality of these elements. But the danger is that we can receive in the next period too much "yeast" for the needs of the party. The disintegration of the Communist Party will very probably *begin* not among the workers but among the intellectuals, who are more sensitive to the ideas and less loyal to the organization. The influx of the new generation of intellectuals to the Communist Party will stop even before the open disintegration of the Stalinist organization. Because of this we can wait for an influx of fresh intellectual elements toward us. Our party can be inundated by nonproletarian elements and can even lose its revolutionary character. The task is naturally not to prevent the influx of intellectuals by artificial methods (such political Malthusianism would be at least premature) but to orient in practice the whole organization toward the factories, the strikes, the unions. It seems that this should be one of the most important tasks of the new convention, if not in an open session then in a closed commission or section work with virtual participation of all the delegates.

The orientation of the whole party toward factory work is intimately connected with the question of the organizational structure of the party. I don't believe that in view of the very small number of our members and the very short experience in mass work, we could establish emphatic rules for the party organization now. We must leave some elbow room for the local organizations. As to the National Committee itself, in order to improvise, adapt, and select the most adequate methods and forms in approaching our new tasks, it would be fatal to imitate a big party with its established forms of activity. The worst of all bureaucratisms is the bureaucratism of a small body which sacrifices practical tasks for an imposing appearance. We should not renounce guerrilla methods, but should continue them upon the condition that the National Committee controls and directs this guerrilla activity. A concrete example: We cannot devote enough or equal forces to all the factories. Our local organization can choose for its activity in the next period one, two, or three factories in its area and concentrate all its forces upon these factories. If we have in one of them two or three workers we can create a special help commission of five nonworkers with the purpose of enlarging our influence in these factories.

The same can be done among the trade unions. We cannot introduce nonworker members in workers' unions. But we can with success build up help commissions for oral and literary action in connection with our comrades in the union. The unbreakable conditions should be: not to command the workers but only to help them, to give them suggestions, to arm them with the facts, ideas, factory papers, special leaflets, and so on.

Such collaboration would have a tremendous educational importance from one side for the worker comrades, from the other side for the nonworkers who need a solid reeducation.

You have, for example, an important number of Jewish nonworker elements in your ranks. They can be a very valuable yeast if the party succeeds by and by in extracting them from a closed milieu and tying them to the factory workers by daily activity. I believe such an orientation would also assure a more healthy atmosphere inside the party. Naturally it is not necessary to emphasize that an adequate corresponding part of the Jewish members should concentrate their forces especially to work among the Jewish masses.

The distribution and alignment of our forces should be done, I repeat, not in accordance with some a priori scheme, but in accordance with concrete and concretely conceived tasks in different parts of the country and even of a town. Only one general rule can we establish immediately: a party member who doesn't win during three or six months a new worker for the party is not a good party member.

If we seriously established such a general orientation and if we verified the practical results every week, we would avoid a great danger: namely, that the intellectuals and white-collar workers might suppress the worker minority, condemn it to silence, transform the party into a very intelligent discussion club but absolutely not habitable for workers.

The selection of party functionaries from below to the top should be done under the same criterion. We naturally cannot appoint only workers, even not a majority of workers. Not all workers are suitable for the job. But every functionary must be attentive to what the worker faces and what he needs. Many intellectuals and half-intellectuals terrorize the workers by some abstract generalities and paralyze the will toward activity. A functionary of a revolutionary party should have in the first place a good ear, and only in the second place a good tongue.

You can see that my letter consists two-thirds of abstract "generalities" and that many of them are too elementary. I see it very well myself, but in order to avoid any misunderstanding I prefer to say even superfluities, with the assurance that you understand very well the peculiarities of the position of an observer from afar.

With my best wishes,

Comradely,
Hansen [Trotsky]

P.S.—The same rules should be in a corresponding form elaborated for the working and recruiting of the youth organization, otherwise we run the danger of educating good young elements into revolutionary dilettantes and not revolutionary fighters.

EXCERPT FROM LETTER ON AMERICAN PROBLEMS

November 14, 1937

Dear Comrade Cannon:

. . . I hear from some comrades that the mood in your ranks is a bit "pessimistic" and only a minority is really active. Possibly it is only a transitional phenomenon corresponding to the passage from one form of activity to another. But it is also possible that a number of good comrades who have been with us almost ten years are a bit tired at the too slow development of the organization. I have observed analogous phenomena many times. In this case it is necessary to introduce fresh blood into all the leading bodies of the party and generally select systematically young elements for the party cadres.

I am very interested in the position of comrades on the USSR matter. The sentimental reaction against the indescribable crimes of the bureaucracy in the USSR, in Spain, and elsewhere and its counterrevolutionary role in the international working class movement generally must inevitably influence the sociological and psychological appreciation of the USSR. I believe we should remain firm on this question but also be pedagogically tolerant to the inevitable exaggerations in our own ranks. We have the possibility of wielding a club against the Oehlerites and other people of the same kind outside the party. I am ready to write an article on this question for the *Socialist Appeal* if you send me the necessary Oehlerite, anarchist, and similar material.

Hansen [Trotsky]

ON DEMOCRATIC CENTRALISM
A Few Words about the Party Regime

December 8, 1937

To the Editors of *Socialist Appeal:*

During the past months I have received letters in regard to the inner regime of a revolutionary party from several apparently young comrades, unknown to me. Some of these letters complain about the "lack of democracy" in your organization, about the domineering of the "leaders" and the like. Individual comrades ask me to give a "clear and exact formula on democratic centralism" which would preclude false interpretations.

It is not easy to answer these letters. Not one of my correspondents even attempts to demonstrate clearly and concretely with actual examples exactly wherein lies the violation of democracy. On the other hand, insofar as I, a bystander, can judge on the basis of your newspaper and your bulletins, the discussion in your organization is being conducted with full freedom. The bulletins are filled chiefly by representatives of a tiny minority. I have been told that the same holds true of your discussion meetings. The decisions are not yet carried out. Evidently they will be carried through at a freely elected conference. In what then could the violations of democracy have been manifested? This is hard to understand. Sometimes, to judge by the tones of the letters, i.e., in the main instance by the formlessness of the grievances, it seems to be that the complainers are simply dissatisfied with the fact that in spite of the existing democracy, they prove to be in a tiny minority. Through my own experience I know that this is unpleasant. But wherein is there any violation of democracy?

Neither do I think that I can give such a formula on democratic centralism that "once and for all" would eliminate misunderstandings and false interpretations. A party is an active organism. It develops in the struggle with outside obstacles and inner contradictions. The malignant decomposition of the Second and Third Internationals, under the severe conditions of the imperialist epoch, creates for the Fourth International difficulties unprecedented in history. One cannot overcome them with some sort of magic formula. The regime of a party does not fall ready-made from the sky but is formed gradually in the struggle. A political line predominates over the regime. First of all, it is necessary to define strategic problems and tactical methods correctly in order to solve them. The organizational forms should correspond to the strategy and the tactic. Only a correct policy can guarantee a healthy party regime. This, it is understood, does not mean that the development of the party does not raise organizational problems as such. But it means that the formula for democratic centralism must inevitably find a different expression in the parties of different countries and in different stages of development of one and the same party.

Democracy and centralism do not at all find themselves in an invariable ratio to one another. Everything depends on the concrete circumstances, on the political situation in the country, on the strength of the party and its experience, on the general level of its members, on the authority the leadership has succeeded in winning. Before a conference, when the problem is one of formulating a political line for the next period, democracy triumphs over centralism. When the problem is political action, centralism subordinates democracy to itself. Democracy again asserts its rights when the party feels the need to examine critically its own actions. The equilibrium between democracy and centralism establishes itself in the actual struggle, at moments it is violated and then again reestablished. The maturity of each member of the party expresses itself particularly in the fact that he does not demand from the party regime more than it can give. The person who defines his attitude to the party by the individual fillips that he gets on the nose is a poor revolutionist. It is necessary, of course, to fight against every individual mistake of the leadership, every injustice, and the like. But it is necessary to assess these "injustices" and "mistakes" not by themselves but in connection with the general development of the party both on a national and international scale. A correct judgment and feeling for proportion in politics is an extremely important thing. The person who has propensities for making a mountain out of a molehill can do much harm to himself and to the party. The misfortune of such people as Oehler, Field, Weisbord, and others consists in their lack of feeling for proportion.

At the moment there are not a few half-revolutionists, tired out by defeats, fearing difficulties, aged young men who have more doubts and pretensions than will to struggle. Instead of seriously analyzing political questions in essence, such individuals seek panaceas, on every occasion complain about the "regime," demand wonders from the leadership, or try to muffle their inner skepticism by ultraleft prattling. I fear that revolutionists will not be made out of such elements, unless they take themselves in hand. I do not doubt, on the other hand, that the young generation of workers will be capable of evaluating the programmatic and strategical content of the Fourth International according to merit and will rally to its banner in ever greater numbers. Each real revolutionist who notes down the blunders of the party regime should first of all say to himself: "We must bring into the party a dozen new workers!" The young workers will call the gentlemen-skeptics, grievance-mongers, and pessimists to order. Only along such a road will a strong healthy party regime be established in the sections of the Fourth International.

L. Trotsky

FINANCING THE REVOLUTIONARY MOVEMENT

July 23, 1938

. . . I have the impression that our practical methods of action are not in accordance with our revolutionary program, that we are too passive in our practical activity. It is not only a question concerning the fascist danger or the question of activity in the trade unions, but also in such matters as the publishing of our paper and our whole activity. I cannot understand how this very revolutionary YPSL organization is not capable of publishing the *Challenge* once a month. It is due to financial difficulties. I absolutely cannot understand why.

In Paris during the war we published a daily paper beginning with a capital of thirty francs ($8.00) and we published it for almost three years. How? We had three devoted comrades in a printing shop, and they worked it. When we had money, we paid them. When we had no money, they waited for better times. I believe that at least our young comrades should make the same effort, not only to have a central printing shop in New York, but one in every important region, such as we had in czarist Russia in every important town. We must have such printing shops if we have nothing else. For example, our English comrades now have their own printing shop, but to have such a printing shop with two or three devoted comrades, we can put out not only the *Socialist Appeal* at least twice a week, but also pamphlets, leaflets, etc. The trouble is that the party work is too much based on petty-bourgeois conceptions.

We must educate our youth for more of a spirit of sacrifice. We already have so many young bureaucrats in our movement. For example, the *Challenge* needs $300. If they lack it, good, they wait. That is not the revolutionary way. It is a very opportunistic policy, far more opportunistic than advocating a labor party. You know that the reason we don't have the revolution is because the workers are held back by bourgeois prejudices—democratic prejudices. We don't have these prejudices, but in the matter of approaching practical things we have the bourgeois manner. It is very useful for the bourgeois class.

The American workers consider it a degradation not to have a Ford, fine clothes, for they think they must do the same as the bourgeois. It is disgraceful to imitate the upper class. We Marxists understand this very well. Absolutely bad, in a revolutionary situation particularly. But in practical methods we act the same way. We don't have the revolutionary courage to break this tradition, to break the bourgeois norms of conduct and set up our own rules of moral duty, etc. This is especially true for youth, and it is extremely important, not only to educate themselves theoretically, but to educate themselves as militants, as men and women.

PROBLEMS OF THE AMERICAN PARTY

October 5, 1938

Dear Friend:

We wait here with the greatest impatience for information about the meeting in Europe. We know only that it was O.K., but no more. Without waiting for your letter, I will discuss with you some questions concerning our party (SWP).

1. The referendum seems to have been not a very happy invention. The discussion seems to have produced some embarrassment in the party. This can all be overcome only by *action*. It is time, it seems to me, to show directly to the party how we have to act on this issue. I had two long discussions here with Plodkin, an organizer of the [International] Ladies Garment Workers Union, and summarized our discussion in an article which tries to put the question on its actual political level. The article is now under translation and will be sent to you simultaneously with this letter. But an article is of course nothing if the party doesn't begin a serious action in the unions with the slogan that the workers should take the state into their own hands and that for this purpose they need their own independent labor party. An energetic step in this direction would surely dissipate all the misunderstandings and dissatisfactions and push the party forward.

2. In this question as in all others it is absolutely necessary to give to our propaganda-agitation a more concentrated and systematic character. It would be for example necessary to oblige all local committees to present to the National Committee in one month a short report concerning their connections with the trade unions, the possibilities for work in trade unions, and especially the agitation in the trade unions for an independent labor party. The danger is that the question of the labor party will become a pure abstraction. The base for our activity is the trade unions—the question of the labor party can receive flesh and blood only insofar as we are rooted in the trade unions. A serious beginning of our work in the trade unions led us to the slogan of a labor party. Now it is necessary to use the slogan of labor party in order to push our party more deeply into the trade unions.

The answers of the local organizations should be studied and worked out in a series of articles and circular letters of the National Committee with concrete instructions, advice, and so on.

3. Very important in this respect is the attitude of the *Socialist Appeal*. It is undoubtedly a very good Marxist paper, but it is as yet not a genuine instrument of political action. The connection of the paper with the real activity of the party is too loose. This looseness is determined not so much by the literary conceptions of the editorial board as by the disseminated, unconcentrated character of the activity of the whole party. It is necessary to establish for a certain time a plan for a political campaign and to subordinate to this plan the local organizations, the *Socialist Appeal*, and the *New International*. It seems to us here that the labor party can be one of the items of such a campaign under the condition that the accent is put on our work in the trade unions.

4. We here were disappointed by the inexplicable passivity of our party towards the patriotic, imperialistic turn of the Communist Party. The greatest hindrance for the revolutionary movement and through this the greatest hindrance for the development of our party and its success in the unions is undoubtedly Stalinism. The fight

against this perfidious enemy of the proletariat should be conducted simultaneously on different levels by combined means. The investigation of the Dies Committee gave us an excellent occasion for action, but this occasion remained almost totally unexploited. We should have defended energetically and ardently the right of the Communist Party to be non-American; it was our elementary democratic duty. At the same time it was necessary to unmask their perfidious turn from a non-American (internationalist) position to an American (chauvinist) one. It was absolutely necessary to arm every member of our party with quotations from the resolutions and the program of the Comintern and its first four, even six, congresses, and to oppose to these documents the recent declarations, speeches, and so on. This work should have been done in a very systematic, detailed form, with two or three articles in every issue of the *Socialist Appeal*, with more synthetic articles in the *New International*, with a special manual for our agitators including quotations, instructions, and so on. I tried to interest the editorial board of the *Socialist Appeal* in this question, but without success. They gave something about the matter (from Olgin's articles) but nothing more. I believe this grave omission could be rectified now to a certain degree. Such a concentrated and systematic campaign could be fixed for two or three months and have the greatest educational value for our own comrades, especially the youth. It is also one of the ways to prepare them for the approaching war.

5. Don't you believe that it would be timely now to create a special party committee for work among the women, with a special supplement of the *Socialist Appeal* and some articles in the *New International* illuminating the situation of worker women now under the crisis?

I will await with great interest your letter on the international meeting as well as on the state of our party as you found it upon your return.

With best greetings,

Comradely,
Hansen [Trotsky]

FOR A COURAGEOUS REORIENTATION

June 16, 1939

Dear Friend:

I have just received Goldman's letter. Concerning the Marxist center, it is a purely tactical question and I believe we can give the IS full freedom in maneuvering on this question. I see no principled objection to a repetition of the experiment of direct contact with the centrists busy with the creation of the new international. Our representatives can lose nothing and gain something if they are firm in the essence and elastic in the form.

The prewar situation, the aggravation of nationalism, and so on, is a natural hindrance to our development and the profound cause of the depression in our ranks. But it must now be underlined that the more the party is petty bourgeois in its composition, the more it is dependent upon the changes in the official public opinion. It is a supplementary argument for the necessity for a courageous and active reorientation toward the masses. (The Negro question takes on a new importance. The Negroes will hardly be patriotic in the coming war.)

The pessimistic reasonings you mention in your article are, of course, a reflection of the patriotic, nationalistic pressure of the official public opinion. "If fascism is victorious in France . . . ," "if fascism is victorious in England . . . ," and so on. The victories of fascism are important, but the death agony of capitalism is more important. Fascism accelerates the new war and the new war will tremendously accelerate the revolutionary movement. In case of war every small revolutionary nucleus can and will become a decisive, historic factor in a very short time. It is shameful that revolutionaries see only one side of the present historic development—its dark, reactionary side—and ignore the approach of a general denouement in which the Fourth International will have the same role to play as did the Bolsheviks in 1917.

Comradely,
Trotsky

REPORT ON THE FOUNDING CONVENTION OF THE SOCIALIST WORKERS PARTY

by James P. Cannon

February 1938

To the International Secretariat,
Dear Comrades,

By this time you will have received the minutes of the National Convention. This will give you the possibility of checking over the work done there more precisely.

Here I want to give you a few personal impressions which you can take together with the reports you have heard from other comrades and eventually arrive at a general impression of your own.

1. *Representation*: According to the final report of the credentials committee we had 76 regular delegates, 37 alternate delegates, and 24 fraternal delegates. This makes a total of 137. In addition, I estimate, there were a couple of score of comrades and very close sympathizers from other cities who were admitted into the convention sessions. The delegates came from 35 cities in seventeen states. From these figures one can get a fairly clear impression that our organization, despite its comparatively small size, is spreading out over the country and has already the fairly good framework of a national organization. In this respect—which I consider very important for the future—we have long outstripped the Lovestoneites for example, who remain primarily a New York group. The same is true of all the other groups and cliques with which we have had conflicts in the past. Among all the radical groupings ours alone is developing a really national composition.

2. *Composition of the Convention*: Precise statistics of the social composition, age, and background of the convention delegates were not compiled, unfortunately. This was contemplated but over-looked in the rush of things. However, I can state that the large majority of the delegates were proletarian activists and trade unionists. Not only that, the work of the Trade Union Commission and the discussion of the trade union question showed that we have a large number of comrades, sufficiently experienced and qualified in mass work, to be able to discuss all sides of the trade union question, including its most practical aspects, with the fullest assurance, as a result of their experience. I think the composition, and general character of the convention, must prompt you to make a certain revision in previous impressions of the composition and general character of the party membership, which it seems to me you entertained. Tourists and letter-writers can give certain impressions of the American movement, and valuable and necessary ones too. But these impressions by no means are representative of the party and the movement, as a whole. The proletarian activists, as a rule, do not have the time and the means for extensive travel. And as a rule their correspondence is confined to laconic reports. One can also get a one-sided impression of the party from the Chicago and New York organizations, which, despite their merits, have serious shortcomings on the side of social composition and trade union activity. It is necessary to see the party as a whole, in a representative convention, to get a clear picture of what it is made of.

3. *International*: This point on the agenda did not provoke very much discussion. This can be accounted for, to a certain extent, by the fact that no differences of opinion were manifested. The decision to affiliate to the Bureau of the Fourth International was unanimous and likewise the provision to apportion a definite percentage of the party dues to International Bureau expenses met with universal approval. It was interesting to note, especially on this point, that the divisions between the old cadres of the Workers Party and the cadres of "native" Socialists have pretty well

been obliterated in the course of a common work and discussion. Such objections and reservations on the question of 100% "Trotskyism" as we have encountered, have come from individuals of the older cadre and not from the former Socialists. I do not at all wish to maintain that the party is thoroughly internationalized. But theoretically the victory on this score is already complete in the united organization.

4. *Orientation*: The convention showed quite clearly that the orientation toward mass work, which began at the time of the French turn, has developed quite consistently. I think it can be said that more progress has been made up till now, in this respect, in the ranks than in the leadership. While it is true that the general lead was given by the National Committee, the delegates more or less ran away with this issue and gave it real life at the convention. During the year or so of our work in the Socialist Party, the leadership put too narrow a construction on the purely factional side of this work and tended to overlook the coordination of the internal faction work with practical activity in the class struggle on a broader scale. Of course, I'm stating here my personal opinion but I do not make much of a secret of it. I consider the leadership on the whole has been very remiss during the past year in this respect, especially during the periods of our intense preoccupation with the internal struggle.

However, the locals and branches, on their own initiative, in various localities developed trade union activity, established contact and broadened their experience and connections in this field. The most hopeful side of the convention revelations, in this respect, was not the work that has already been accomplished but the fact that it was accomplished pretty largely on the initiative of the local comrades themselves. This gives ground to think that with a more decisive orientation on the part of the party as a whole, and with a serious attempt at coordination and centralized direction, we can hope for still more gratifying results in the next period. Two postconvention items give special grounds for encouragement: the first is the result of the elections in the Marine Firemen's Union on the west coast. No doubt you have heard that the progressive slate swept out the Stalinites by a 3 to 2 majority all along the line. The second item was the reinstatement of one of our comrades [Bert Cochran] to his position as International organizer of the automobile workers union at Cleveland. In the reactionary drive of the general executive board of the automobile workers union, he was removed from his position, about three weeks ago. Thereupon the locals in the district raised such a furor, bombarded the national office with so many truculent resolutions of protest, that they were compelled to reinstate him in his position. I think this is a very interesting case. The comrade, who is still a very young man—only 24 years old—got his political education in our New York movement. Then, in the early days of the Workers Party, he was sent out in the field to see what he could do in the line of mass work, without previous experience. The leadership, perhaps, deserves credit for encouraging him to start out on this course. All the rest he did by himself.

5. *Political Firmness*: The discussion and the vote on the principal questions in dispute should be an eye-opener for anyone who thinks that fundamental positions can be lightly discarded in our party. After all the furor that was raised around the Russian question in the preconvention discussion, with all the groups and grouplets that came forward with new revelations in this respect, and despite the fact that a minority of the National Committee came forward with an opposition point of view—despite all this—the convention supported the line of the National Committee with a crushing unanimity. On page 14 of the minutes you will see the record of the vote; for the majority 66, for the N.C. minority 3, for the Glee opposition 2, for a special position of Heisler 1. On page 19 the minutes show the Spanish Resolution adopted by a vote of 56 against 4 abstentions.

It will be interesting for you to study the roll call on the Russian question and see the solid lineup of delegates, delegation after delegation. And they are not routine votes either. There was more than ample preconvention discussion and the delegates showed in the discussion that they understand their positions very clearly. *The various sections of our International, who may have got the impression of deep cleavages over the Russian question from our Internal Bulletin, should be apprised of these votes.*

The decisions of the convention on the disputed questions have naturally had a stabilizing effect on the internal life of the party, and have put a stop completely to discussion and controversy. It appears that most of the comrades who have been in opposition are disposed to let the matter rest now until another period of party work and experience intervenes. On the other hand, it can be said, that the party rank and file are in no mood to tolerate any infringement of the convention decisions. The slightest signs of such a tendency would be dealt with promptly and without ceremony. Although all the opposition tendencies appeared at the convention, more or less, as isolated individuals, nevertheless there was nothing resembling a crushing or terrorizing policy. Everybody who had a dissenting point of view was given ample time to explain his position to the convention, in most cases equal time with the majority reporters. Although we maintained, and still maintain, that advocacy of defeatism with respect to the Soviet Union is incompatible with adherence to our movement for the Fourth International, we found it possible, in view of the unanimity of the convention, to refrain from any organizational measures in this respect. Consequently all the opposition comrades, including even the three or four who defended a defeatist point of view have the opportunity to reflect further on the matter and to adjust themselves to the firmly established position of the party.

6. *Party Democracy*: The action of the convention overruling and censuring the Chicago City Executive Committee in the cases of Becket and Most should be noted. This is recorded in the minutes, under the report of the Grievance Committee, on pages 8, 9, and 10 and again on page 17. Here it was not so much a question of correcting a real injustice, as of insisting on the most scrupulous observation of regularity and formality in disciplinary cases. The convention action gained added force from the fact that the individuals involved, Becket and Most, were without any support whatever in the convention. I consider these decisions very important from the point of view of establishing precedent: that no kind of summary action is to be encouraged in disciplinary matters. The delegates were very "touchy" on this point and did not hesitate to demonstrate it, even though our political friends of the Chicago City Executive Committee were involved and censured.

7. *Leadership*: The convention made a little shake-up in the leadership when it came time to elect the new National Committee. Several comrades who had been members of the committee for two years were eliminated and new forces were added. In one or two cases members of the N.C. were reduced to the ranks of alternates, in other cases, members of the Political Committee were elected to the National Committee but not to the Political Committee this time. In this case also some new blood was infused into the body. Provisions were made for quarterly meetings of the plenum of the National Committee. The Political Committee is to be subject to alteration at each plenum of the N.C. The national staff is strengthened by the addition of a full-time Trade Union Secretary.

In my opinion, these measures were imperatively necessary. Some of them were considered drastic and produced a certain shock. But that is good for the party and also for the individuals concerned, perhaps. Some comrades who are inclined to take a personal view of things have seen in the action of the convention, on this point, only a shuffling of the N.C. slate. However, it had a far profounder meaning. It marks, I hope, the beginning of a process which is to be carried out relentlessly under a slogan: The subordination of the leadership to the ranks. The isolation of a part, at least, of the national leadership from the rank and file of the party, the encumbrance of the leadership with honorary and inactive members, tendency of the leadership to develop into a sort of officers' club whose members never offend or discipline each other, and who are free from the discipline of the ranks—all this sort of thing had developed into a crying evil in the party.

It appeared obvious to me in such a situation that matters could not be remedied by a mere reshuffling of the slate, with the polite agreement of all concerned. It was necessary to deal a blow to the whole system. This could only be done by direct intervention of the active comrades in the ranks themselves. For this reason I declined to participate in the making up of a slate. But I did frankly encourage, and even instigate, the leading proletarian delegations to take matters into their own hands and rearrange the leadership in accordance with merit and activity. I am inclined to think that an error was made here and there in the selection or rejection of this or that individual, but the whole course initiated at the convention was right and salutary.

The necessary transformation from the propaganda circle to the mass work is finding its full reflection only belatedly in the leadership itself. And since the initiative, for a variety of reasons, could not, or at least did not, come through the National Committee, it had to come from below. Perhaps this is best in the end. I look forward to the next convention with the hope that a still more vigorous and determined supervision, and if necessary, overhauling of the leading personnel will take place.

In my judgement, this is the most important question. That the convention delegates showed an alertness to the problem, and a readiness to tackle it head-on, gives me more confidence for the future of the party than anything else. When it becomes clearly apparent to all that the rank-and-file activists are watching the leadership all the time—not merely the leadership as a whole but each individual member of it—and requires of them continuous activity and responsibility, we will be on the road to the eventual selection of a leadership that is worthy of its task. The convention showed very clearly that we have much promising material in the ranks, that we are developing a strong second line of leadership who know how to keep a vigilant and critical eye on those immediately above them, and, if necessary, to substitute for them.

Best wishes,

Fraternally,
National Secretary

P.S. Today's mail brings news of a new branch at New Castle, Pa., and possibly, a new one (from the Stalinists) at East St. Louis, Ill. We are gaining recruits from the Stalinists steadily.

THE TRUTH ABOUT THE AUTO CRISIS:
The Petty-bourgeois Leaders Before the Test of the Class Struggle

By George Clarke

It is now approximately one year since the dispute arose between the New York Political Committee and the comrades in the field over the policy to be followed by party members in the auto workers union—popularly known as the "auto crisis." This event is now history but it is important history in that it serves to illuminate more than any other single incident the real meaning of the current factional struggle.

Shachtman, Burnham, Abern, and the other leaders of the minority have deliberately distorted the facts of the "auto crisis," carefully hidden their true meaning, and laid down a smokescreen composed of the secondary aspects of the crisis which bears no significant relation to the principal issue. There is nothing astonishing in this. They conceal the truth from party members for very substantial personal reasons:

1. The "auto crisis" contains a crushing answer to the charges made by them in their fanciful document "War and Bureaucratic Conservatism";

2. The "auto crisis" reveals that if ever the party leadership was administered in an arrogant, bureaucratic manner it was by Burnham, Shachtman, and Abern;

3. It reveals that their conception of the powers and authority of leadership is one based on *formal* authority and not upon the voluntary confidence and respect granted them by the rank and file for competence in answering the practical problems of the class struggle and solving questions in dispute with skill and understanding;

4. It reveals that the Burnham-Shachtman-Abern leadership was prepared, in a *practical matter,* mind you!, to use the most drastic measures to enforce the formal powers of the P.C., to establish their authority by main force even if it meant disgracing comrades directly involved in an important sector of the class struggle and compromising the party in the eyes of thousands of workers;

5. It revealed in Shachtman and Burnham qualities of stubbornness and capriciousness entirely alien to leaders of a proletarian movement—qualities which made them incapable of making concessions in a *practical matter* except under the most insistent pressure from the most experienced trade unionists in the party and from a whole cadre of loyal, tested, and responsible comrades. And when the concessions were finally made, they showed themselves to be embittered, petulant petty bourgeois, threatening to resign from leadership, washing their hands of all responsibility for the change in policy and for its execution and taunting the comrades in the field with prophecies of disaster. (How differently they react when the fundamentals of the party program are involved! How flexible they are before the pressure of the petty-bourgeois radicals and bourgeois liberals!)

6. It revealed not only an unwillingness to learn from the workers and the trade unionists but a presumptuous attempt to teach in a field where they admittedly are least qualified, least informed, and least experienced; it revealed complete ignorance of the dynamics of the workers' movement—a formalistic, undialectical approach to the real problems of the class struggle.

These charges will be proved beyond the possibility of successful contradiction in this document.* To those not blinded by factional animus, the auto crisis will indicate far more than an incidental error in policy. The auto crisis was, in a sense, a microcosm of the present factional

* All facts concerning meetings where the author was not present have been carefully checked with official documents and participants at the meetings.

struggle—a prophetic warning of the kind of party the SWP would be under the leadership of Burnham-Abern-Shachtman or the kind of party Burnham-Abern-Shachtman will lead outside the ranks of the Fourth International if they carry out their threats of split.

I. THE FAMOUS NEW YEAR'S DAY MEETING

The "auto crisis" has its chronological and psychological origin in what has now become the "notorious" New Year's Day meeting. The opposition has for months been whispering—mostly misinformation—in corridors, cafeterias, and private homes about this "notorious" meeting. The Winchellian masterpiece "War and Bureaucratic Conservatism" assigns prominent place to this meeting. It alleges that this meeting proved that: "The P.C. is in reality a fiction or at best a semi-fiction [!]. Its authority is strictly limited: here it may act, but into this territory it may not venture. Over the P.C. looms the N.C. (which formally is as it should be); and over the N.C. looms the final authority—the Cannon clique. . . . But even the N.C. is largely fictitious. It is called upon to act only rarely [We will soon see how much respect the Burnham-Shachtman-Abern "democrats" actually have for the National Committee—G.C.] and then its deliberations have an air of unreality. The clique itself is the court of last appeal, on all 'crucial' questions—i.e., questions 'of regime.'" And this is illustrated by the January 1 meeting, which sat "as a *deciding* body, usurping the functions of both P.C. and N.C." (*Internal Bulletin*, vol. II, no. 6, pp. 12 and 13).

Now what actually happened? Late in December 1938, Comrades Cannon, Dunne, and Smith had a conversation in Minneapolis concerning trade union matters. In the course of his work Comrade Smith had developed new contacts. The question of how these contacts could be utilized to build our forces in auto was discussed in the Minneapolis meeting of the three comrades and some tentative plans were worked out. It was agreed that Smith would submit the proposals to his contacts; further concrete steps awaited the results. On December 30, Comrade Cannon received a wire from Smith informing him that Smith had made satisfactory agreements with his friends and that he and Dunne would arrive in New York to discuss plans more concretely. Cannon immediately wired Cochran (then in Flint) to come to New York so he could supply information on the auto situation, with which he was conversant.

The first informal meeting between these four comrades took place on New Years Eve. Immense possibilities were opened up for our work in auto. Plans for a large-scale, aggressive campaign were outlined. The Opposition seriously reproaches the out-of-town comrades for the jesting reply made to queries about their appearance at the party affair "that they wanted to attend the New Year's Eve party." What stupidity and nonsense! Do they seriously suggest that information about such a highly confidential mission as this be discussed, or even information given at a New Year's Eve party—of all places? Shachtman, Burnham, and Clarke were, however, asked to attend an informal meeting the next day.

At the session the following day at Cannon's home, a report of the meeting the previous day was given. Proposed plans for the campaign were outlined. The plans were for Cochran to return to Michigan to lead our group in auto; Clarke to go to Detroit for party work and Jules Geller to Flint. Confidential matters relating to the financing of the campaign were discussed. Contrary to Opposition insinuations little discussion took place over policy to be followed in auto—we shall return to this point later. The campaign was to be conducted under the direction of the N.C. members in the field with authority to decide practical questions on the spot. By and large, this is the only way to conduct a serious trade union campaign. Naturally the field committee was not freed of supervision or of final veto by the P.C. The proposed plans were approved by all present for representation, *discussion*, and ratification or *rejection* by the Political Committee. (Incidentally, Felix Morrow was not present at this meeting as the Opposition asserts in its document.)

On January 3 at the Political Committee all members were present, including N.C. members Clarke, Morrow, and Morgan (alternate), and Lebrun and Roberts by invitation. The plans for the campaign were presented as fully as possible by Cannon and accepted by the committee without opposition either in the discussion or in the vote.

The only discordant note was struck by Abern, who was playing his old game of clique politics. He proposed "that Comrade Clarke remain in N.Y. for a period of sixty days to work on the *Appeal*, pending the addition of forces to the *Appeal*; that during the period of sixty days, the labor secretary (Widick) proceed to Michigan to work there, assisting in the party and trade union organizational work." It was of little importance to Abern that Clarke had worked for over a year and a half in the Michigan areas as organizer; knew all the comrades personally and had excellent relations with them; had many contacts among auto workers and was well informed on the problems of the auto union. Abern was concerned, as always, with rewarding a member of his clique for personal loyalty: Give Widick a chance to cop some "glory" in a big campaign! The trick use of the words "labor secretary" in his motion were too obvious a ruse to deceive any of the members of the committee. Abern's amendment was defeated by all votes except those of Abern and Widick (!).

No intimation was given at this meeting or previously that *anyone* had objections to the New Year's consultation or considered it "usurping the functions of both P.C. and N.C." How could there possibly have been objections to this procedure? Scores of such consultations had occurred previously and subsequently among leading members of the party—consultations in which the only member of the so-called "Cannon Clique" present was Cannon himself. Such consultations take place in every serious organization that ever existed.

As a general rule practically all important formal decisions are preceded by informal consultations and discussions in the course of which definitive plans finally take shape. There was nothing wrong in the New Year's meeting nor in the New Year's Eve meeting nor in the preliminary consultations in the field. The comrades involved deserve not criticism but credit for initiating the plans for the campaign and developing them in informal consultations in order to bring them finally before the P.C. in the form of a practical program of action. Practically all important party actions are initiated and developed that way and cannot be efficiently prepared any other way. What the party needs is more comrades who can initiate and develop practical plans for trade union campaigns and bring them before the P.C. for ratification.

Secondly, it should now be clear that highly confidential matters were discussed at the New Year's Day meeting. That was quite clear to the members of the P.C. meeting at that time. There isn't space in this document to relate the numerous occasions when matters requiring secrecy have been discussed by small committees. Nobody ever thought or said in those instances that the failure to call in all P.C. members constituted a "usurping" action. Everyone knew and knows that this method was chosen for the protection of the party from premature or unnecessary exposure.

Then why—the Opposition still asks—were Gould, Abern, Widick, McKinney (the other members of the P.C.) not invited? For two very good reasons besides those stated above:

1. All of those present were personally directly involved in the contemplated activity. Moreover, two other campaigns were already under way (the twice-weekly *Appeal* drive, and the French campaign). Clarke had been the active editor of the *Appeal* up to that time; if he was to leave for Michigan someone had to take his place. Shachtman was unquestionably the indicated person, especially since the twice-weekly would soon be a reality. Cannon was to leave for France shortly. His place in the office had to be filled by someone during his absence. Goldman was suggested but it was indicated that Goldman could not leave Chicago for some time. In the meanwhile, the proposal was made that Shachtman and Burnham take over the office work with the assistance of Abern. All these motions are recorded in the P.C. minutes of January 3.

2. Abern's presence in a meeting where confidential information was reported was considered a disquieting factor. Everyone knew that Abern's clique—consisting of irresponsible people—was always informed of everything that occurred in the P.C, in its formal and informal meetings. Everyone knew that twice before in party history—just prior to fusion with the Musteite American Workers Party and just prior to the split in the SP—confidential information of this kind had fallen into the hands of our enemies. Abern was not trusted, and most of all not trusted by his present caucus comrades. To keep Abern out of the meeting and not create a factional situation—so

we innocently but mistakenly thought—no other comrade regardless of his post either on the P.C. or N.C. or his trustworthiness could be invited to this meeting. Only comrades directly involved in the contemplated activity were called in.

It was a delicate problem. Burnham and Shachtman appreciated it as much no less than did the so-called members of the "Cannon clique." The fact that they found objections to the procedure post factum—"in the Spring," they say—derived from entirely different reasons than objection to the procedure. Their objection today, the raising of this meeting is a piece of the most brazen dishonesty—a cowardly renunciation for factional reasons of an action necessary for party growth and activity.

It may appear that the New Year's meeting occupies an inordinately long space in this document, entirely out of all proportion to its real importance. But the reader must remember that it is not the so-called "Cannon clique" which put the New Year's meeting on the agenda of the party discussion. This question has been persistently raised by the Opposition, and yet, strangely enough, these champions of "truth" and "morals" deliberately fail to mention the most vital "truth" which emerged at this meeting.

Following reports and discussion of the situation in Michigan, of the technical and financial aspects of the campaign, the meeting turned its attention to personnel. Clarke agreed to leave N.Y. for the post of Detroit organizer, and Cochran to return to Michigan. As a matter of course, Shachtman was asked to assume full-time duty as editor of the *Appeal*. To the great stupefaction of all, Shachtman declined the "nomination." Then with one of his characteristic speeches—where he tries to anticipate objections by admitting guilt in advance—Shachtman declared his intention of quitting full time party work to seek a job in private industry. He had personal difficulties and needed more income. The campaign in auto, the drive for the twice-weekly *Appeal*, the intervention in France would remove Cannon from the center—all of this Shachtman had subordinated to his personal problem. More important, his desertion of full-time work at this crucial moment would have jeopardized those campaigns, to the great detriment of the progress of the party.

Shachtman was aware of all this. Perhaps Shachtman believed he was confronted with a group of hard-boiled, callous fanatics for whom personal problems do not and cannot exist. If he actually entertained any such incredible notion, he was quickly disillusioned. True the comrades were infuriated by Shachtman's announcement of desertion—but they suppressed this anger to suggest financial arrangements that would provide a solution for his personal problem within the movement. The top party wage of $30.00 per week was offered him and it was explained how this wage could be guaranteed. Still Shachtman remained adamant in his declination. Finally, after men like Cannon, Dunne, and Dobbs made speech after speech imploring and begging Shachtman to consent, he said he would "think it over" and give his answer within the next two days.

At the P.C. meeting of January 3, Shachtman accepted the proposal but made sure to couple it with the threat that he was serving notice that the first time the money failed to be paid he would leave the editorship for an outside job. Significantly enough, Burnham never uttered a solitary word during the discussion of Shachtman's role. Undoubtedly he was acting on a principle—the principle that the party has no right to interfere in the personal lives of its leaders; no right to ask them to subordinate their personal problems to the needs of the movement; no right to demand sacrifices from them in a crucial situation. How must the worker feel towards a party which asks him to sacrifice his life in a strike or demonstration and yet considers the serene calm of the lives of its petty-bourgeois leaders a realm which it dare not disturb?

That revolting picture of Shachtman, the professional revolutionist, threatening to desert his post in time of crisis, left an indelible impression in the minds of the witnesses on the scene. If Shachtman would know what single incident, more than anything else, weakened nay, almost shattered our confidence in him, let him turn back to the New Year's Day meeting. If Shachtman would know the historical precedents for his petty-bourgeois tendency—precedent XII added to the chain of eleven irrefutable and annihilating precedents cited by Comrade Trotsky—let him turn back to the New Year's Day meeting.

II. SHACHTMAN-BURNHAM REVERSE THE POLICY OF THE FIELD

Clarke arrived in Detroit on Monday, January 16. By that time the factional struggle between Martin and the Stalinists had once again broken violently into the open. The press was full of charges and counter-charges. The atmosphere was tense and it was obvious that this was the show-down struggle. Clarke discussed at length with the local auto worker comrades their impressions of the struggle and heard their suggestions for party policy. The next day and the day after, the discussions continued in Flint between Cochran, Clarke, Jules Geller, the Johnsons, and Adams, leading party unionist in Michigan on a union assignment. The policy agreed upon was: an attack on both Martin and the Stalinists; a campaign which centered its main emphasis on the unity of the UAW against both groups; and the formation of a Third Group, with a positive program of union action, as the vehicle for this campaign. The question of which convention (Detroit or Cleveland) we would support was left unanswered as not vital to the main line, and as dependent on events which were developing with terrific speed but in an undetermined direction. We will discuss the validity of this or that policy later on in this document. Here we wish merely to state the facts. Smith was contacted by long distance wire and he indicated essential agreement with the policy. For practical reasons, it was impossible to contact Comrade Dunne.

A decision was adopted to summon a national auto conference to discuss the policy outlined above. On Sunday, January 26, auto workers and comrades active in the auto centers in Detroit, Flint, Toledo, Cleveland, and South Bend gathered in Detroit. After a lengthy, lively discussion, in which almost every comrade took part, the policy and proposed program of the Third Group submitted to the conference were unanimously adopted. The comrades left for their home towns full of enthusiasm for the plan of action and eager to get the campaign under way.

Late that night in consultation with Comrades Cochran and Adams, Clark wrote a combined policy-article and news-story for the *Appeal* and mailed it airmail special delivery to N.Y. A copy of the same article was also mailed to Dunne in Minneapolis. The article was purposely vague about the Cleveland and Detroit conventions in line with the policy adopted at the conference that afternoon. Its main fire was directed against both Martin and the Stalinists as splitters. Its slogan was unity. Its method the intervention of the rank and file. The entire policy was summed up in the opening sentences.

"Detroit, Jan. 23—The United Automobile Workers of America, which fought and defeated the biggest monopolies in the country, is now being split wide open by two contenders for power.

"Unless the rank and file speaks up, and speaks up soon, the union will be a smoking ruin, powerless to fight the corporations, unable to shield the interests of the unemployed. The entire labor movement will suffer a major disaster.

"On the one side, is the 'Executive Board Majority,' consisting of the union-wrecking Communist Party-Unity Group crowd in alliance with reactionaries who formerly supported Martin. On the other side is the Martin group, composed of a few bottom-heavy office-holders and backed by a very smelly alliance of reactionaries and Lovestoneites. . . ."

This article—more accurately, the policy contained therein—encountered violent opposition from the leading comrades in N.Y. (*It must be pointed out here that Comrade Cannon had already left for France and did not return to N.Y. until summer, long after the auto dispute had subsided. The P.C. was entirely free from the direct influence of any member of the "Cannon clique" and under the immediate leadership of Burnham-Shachtman.*) Confronted with this sharp disagreement over trade union policy with leading comrades in the field, how did this "leadership" react?

Immediately Burnham sat down at his typewriter and banged out an editorial diametrically opposite in line from that proposed by the article summarizing the policy adopted by the Field Committee and the National Auto Conference. The main line of the Burnham editorial read as follows:

"They [the Stalinists] have now taken their final step. Fearing with good reason to face a really democratic and representative convention of the rank and file of the entire union, they have forced a split of the executive board and called their stooge convention in Cleveland. . . .

"The future of the union movement in auto does not and cannot lie with the Cleveland puppet-show. . . .

"It is time for the militant and progressive rank and file of the U.A.W. to assert *their own rights,* to take over *their union* in *their own name.* The locals must elect their delegates to the Detroit [Martin] convention, not to submit to Martin but to re-establish the rule of the members over their own union."!!

The orientation of this editorial was clearly for the Martin convention, as can be seen, despite the severe condemnation of Martin's policy and the call for the formation of a Third Group. Burnham did one more revealing thing in his editorial which exposes the ultimatistic attitude of the cloistered intellectual towards the workers. The editorial closed with a specific eight-point program for the Third Group to adopt. Clarke's article deliberately left the program in general terms so that it could be issued for the first time *not by the S.W.P. or by the Socialist Appeal,* but by the *Third Group,* which was already in process of formation. We wanted the program to appear as the product of an independent group of auto workers. Burnham apparently wanted to dictate it to the workers—no doubt in the interests of "science" and "truth." One more bureaucratic stunt these "sensitive," "democratic" leaders pulled before they entered the P.C. meeting. They revised Clarke's article—*Bowdlerized* is a better word—in just enough places to completely change its meaning to the exact opposite of what it had originally said. This must have been the work of Shachtman, who has shown himself quite adept at using the same arguments to support diametrically contrary policies. How interesting is the comparison between the brutal way they treated an article from the field and the loud complaints they fill P.C. meetings with when as much as a shade of a meaning of the precious literati Burnham, Shachtman, MacDonald, and Company is changed!

The Political Committee minutes of January 24, 1939, read as follows:

"Article by Clarke on the auto situation read.

"Editorial by Burnham read.

"Motions by Burnham: (1) To adopt the main line of the editorial prepared by Burnham on the UAW as embodying our policy; (2) to revise the article of Comrade Clarke in accordance with the line of the editorial; (3) to publish the editorial and revised article in the current issue of the *Appeal.* Carried.

"General discussion on motion and auto policy."

Observe here (and this is two-thirds of the recorded minutes, the remainder will be quoted later) that there is no motion, no suggestion, no intimation that before adopting a policy completely at loggerheads with the Field Committee and the National Auto Conference, the committee was in the slightest degree interested in gaining additional information from the comrades on the scene. Not even a hint that some P.C. comrade, or the entire P.C, might go out to the field to get information and debate the policy; not even a hint that one of the field comrades might be called into N.Y. for the same purpose—no! these thoughts didn't even enter the minds of Burnham's "democrats." Even the simple proposal that no article, or just a general news story, appear in the next edition of the *Appeal* until a more thorough and rounded discussion could be held with the field comrades seemed as remote as Burnham's present connection with our movement.

The Political Committee, five out of seven members present, was granted the formal right by the National Committee to make decisions between its plenary meetings. Burnham and Company were bureaucratically insisting upon this formal right in a practical trade union matter 700 miles from the scene of action without consultation of the comrades involved and in direct opposition to the desires and policy elaborated by these comrades. They knew, moreover, that comrades from five cities had met and endorsed the field policy. They had been informed in a letter to Shachtman accompanying the article by Clarke. They argue today that Clarke was remiss in his duties for not sending more elaborate information to the P.C. Suppose that is true (although there were extenuating circumstances—constant meetings with auto workers, with our own comrades, and the beginnings of work in a new situation) does that thereby give this committee the prerogative to act like peeved school children and say: "Since you failed to supply us with information we will not ask you for any and we will adopt a policy without your information and against your line." In our movement, this procedure goes by the name of "revenge politics"—the characteristic of petty-bourgeois leaders.

Still, to carry through the policy without consulting the field comrades was a little too brazen even for "daring" generals. A discussion ensued, opened by L. [Lewit], an N.C. member not on the P.C, over somebody going to Detroit for consultation. How did Burnham and Company regard the proposal for consultation? To iron out a common policy? To obtain information? If the discussion at the P.C. meeting had any meaning at all, it was to the effect that the P.C. member would go to the field to put the P.C. line over on the field comrades. Here is how the minutes read:

"Motion by Abern: That Comrade Widick go to Detroit and Dunne come there from Minneapolis.

"Amendment by Burnham: That Shachtman go instead of Widick. Carried. Widick recorded against.

"MEETING ADJOURNED."

An instructive little scene. An exhibition in miniature, in a practical action, of the basic characteristics of the Minority combination as revealed in the present internal struggle.

1. Burnham, the father of the policy and the maker of the motion on the policy does not volunteer to go. He proposes to send instead an errand boy (Shachtman). And nobody even proposes Burnham. Burnham, you see, is the aristocrat of the committee: he does the brain work; the "dirty job" of going out into the field, of persuading comrades of a policy or of carrying it out is not within the province of his class.

2. Abern proposes Widick. Why Widick? Could Widick even convince a Yipsel of a policy he didn't believe in? Could Widick even convey information correctly if he was in disagreement with it? It is not easy to give an affirmative answer to this question. But Widick is a member of Abern's clique—if the boy couldn't go for the "glory" originally, let him go now to teach these insolent "Cannonites" their place. The vote is taken. Nobody is for Widick but Widick himself (and why not? Wasn't Widick labor secretary?). Poor Widick! If only he had half as much ability as conceit!

Just before Shachtman boarded the plane for Detroit, the committee made a final gesture of disregard and contempt for the field comrades: The technical editor of the *Appeal* locked up the forms of the paper containing Burnham's pro-Martin editorial and Clarke's bowdlerized article and prepared it for the press! Evidently to make an agreement easier.

III. SHACHTMAN UP IN THE AIR

Early Tuesday morning, January 25, Shachtman arrived in Detroit. The same afternoon Dunne came by train from Minneapolis. Smith could not attend because of important union business. Discussions began almost immediately, with Dunne, Shachtman, Clarke, and Cochran participating, and continued for more than five hours without interruption. Shachtman came to Detroit, if the unanimous decision of the P.C. means anything, as a defender of the Burnham policy for which he had voted. But Shachtman made no attempt to convince us of the correctness of this policy. He confined himself to questions arising from doubts in his own mind, to questions Shachtman's hypothetical "worker" was liable to ask, to abrupt demands for "yes" and "no" answers to "concrete" questions, to speculations about the future of the labor movement, to precedents of all varieties. Shachtman had no firm, independent position of his own. A poor attorney for Burnham, he was firmly convinced only of his own "doubts." By ten or eleven o'clock that night, in the opinion of all the others Shachtman was ready to change his position in favor of that of the field comrades. He was already seeking answers to questions people like Burnham might ask about their line. But just around that time, Comrade Adams entered the room with a copy of the morning edition of the Detroit Free Press carrying the headline: "MARTIN BOLTS CIO." Dunne was the first to speak on this drastic turn in events. He pointed out that now we must turn our line sharply in favor of the Cleveland CIO convention. The majority of the auto workers favored the CIO and despised the AFL in which direction Martin was now turning. Any other policy would cut us adrift from the main stream of the auto workers movement and isolate us together with an insignificant minority in the Martin group.

With the speed of a recoiling spring, Shachtman seized upon the position outlined by Dunne. Yes, he was for it wholeheartedly. It seemed he was heaving a sigh of relief at returning to his taskmasters in N.Y. with a position unlike either that of Burnham or the original policy of the Field Committee. Unfortunately for Shachtman, however, Clarke and Cochran could not fail to see the logic of Dunne's remarks and quickly arrived at agreement with the new policy. (Later it will be demonstrated that the pro-CIO convention orientation was a modification of the Field Committee line and did not clash with it as it did with the Burnham policy.) In reality Shachtman was not convinced of the pro-CIO convention line any more than he had been convinced of the pro-Martin line.

A good part of the discussion was devoted, on Shachtman's insistence, to an organization question: Did the Field Committee have an "independent" or merely "autonomous" powers? Shachtman accepted our assurances that we wanted no "independence" from the P.C, that we were entirely prepared as a matter of course to be subordinated to it, that we wanted only the "autonomy" the P.C. had unanimously voted us in its January 3 meeting to formulate tactics on the spot without prior consent of the P.C—all of these earnest assurances were accepted by him with considerable skepticism.

Before the meeting broke up Shachtman tried to prevail upon one of us to return to N.Y. to help convince the P.C. of the new line. But this was out of the question because of pressure of the work. All the way down to the airport Shachtman kept trying to convince one of us to return with him and constantly repeating: "I wish I were as sure as you are that your policy is correct." But the discussion was over and Hamlet Shachtman went up in the air again.

IV. BURNHAM CRACKS THE BUREAUCRATIC WHIP

Shachtman reported the position he had taken in agreement with the Field Committee to the P.C. the next day. (The minutes report all present with the exception of Cannon "(out of town)" and Gould "(ill)." Morrow and L. were also present as N.C. members. Shachtman appeared at this meeting, according to the testimony of both L. and Morrow, not as a partisan battling for his convictions but rather as a reporter retailing information. The vehemence and drive with which Shachtman is now trying to change the party's position on its fundamental Marxist doctrine can be compared with his attitude at that meeting only by likening it to the harsh unmeasured tones with which the petty-bourgeois radical lashes at the "extremist" Bolsheviks and his gentle, chiding words admonishing the reactionary bourgeoisie. How could it be otherwise? Within a period of 48 hours Shachtman had taken two basically contradictory positions. He had been equally convinced of each of them—more accurately, equally skeptical of both. Unconvinced himself, how could he possibly convince others? Yet, the facts of the auto situation Shachtman had presented in his report were so persuasive that McKinney and L. came to agreement with the Pro-CIO convention orientation before Shachtman's return from Detroit.

The Committee minutes read as follows:

"SPECIAL P.C. MEETING, January 26, 1939

"Report by Shachtman on the Detroit conference and policies recommended on the UAW.

"Extended discussion on auto policy.

"Motion by Shachtman: That the material in the *Socialist Appeal* be revised before distribution as follows: (1) The latest declaration of Martin is a reactionary step representing a split from the CIO to the AF of L, that is, from the main stream of the militant, progressive, industrial union movement and in capitulation to the AF of L machine, leaving behind in the ranks of the CIO the bulk of the organized workers involved; (2) We must point out that the Stalinists bear the main responsibility for driving the progressive elements in the Martin ranks to an extreme and unsupportable reaction to their provocations; (3) *We stand, at the present stage, for unity inside the CIO, not excluding the variant of a future Martin union converting its present minority into a decisive majority;* (4) In orienting on the Cleveland convention, we call on the members to go there to fight against the Stalinist record, program, and leadership. [My emphasis—G.C.]

"For 1; Against 2; *Abern not voting;* McKinney abstaining. [My emphasis—G.C.]

"Motion by Burnham: To reaffirm the position taken Tuesday. For 3 (Burnham, Widick, Abern); Against 2 (Shachtman, McKinney).

"Motion by McKinney: That the article in the *Socialist Appeal* on the automobile situation be revised along the following lines:

1. To support the Cleveland convention on the ground that the majority of the automobile workers will go to Cleveland since this will be the official CIO convention. This is in line with the position of the party for support of the CIO in preference to the AF of L.

2. The resignation of Martin from the National Council of the CIO is a backward step away from the CIO and logically leads toward the AF of L.

3. The workers of Cleveland must be warned that the Stalinists bear the main responsibility for the difficulties that have arisen in the UAW despite the fact that Martin's course has not been one that would make for unity and a militant union.

4. The Cleveland convention must understand that the automobile workers must institute a struggle against the Stalinist wreckers and drive them from the union.

For 2 (McKinney, Shachtman); Against 2 (Widick, Burnham); *Abern not voting.* L. . . . N.C. Consultative vote for McKinney motion. [My emphasis—G.C.]

"MEETING ADJOURNED"

In comparing the two motions it is obvious from the underlined sections in Shachtman's motion that McKinney's position was far from positive and much less equivocal. Here again the actions of people are more revealing and instructive than all the speeches about themselves:

Widick votes against. His toes had been stepped on and now he is getting his revenge on the "Cannon clique."

Abern abstains from taking a position as he does on all political questions so he can be freed to make any organizational combination the needs of the moment dictate. His vote—"not voting"—is the decisive ballot defeating the McKinney motion. (In the February 7 P.C. meeting Abern corrects the minutes to the effect that he should have been "recorded as voting against both motions." This is a patent fraud. First the secretary could not possibly have recorded him incorrectly on both motions. And second, this weasel device "not voting" is a method almost distinctively peculiar to Abern. The minutes of the P.C. contain innumerable examples of Abern "not voting." By his abstentionist vote Abern was freeing his hands for a bloc with Burnham. His vote reaffirming the Tuesday position commits Abern only to a policy made prior to the hearing of evidence, but it is cancelled out by "not voting" on the other motions. Thus Abern is, as usual, committed only to persons but not to policies.

Burnham remains adamant. None of the overwhelming facts presented by Shachtman had the slightest effect upon him. Nor did the position of as outstanding a trade unionist and responsible party leader as Vincent Dunne. Nor the conversion of Shachtman to the position of the Field Committee. Nor the fact that L. . . . and McKinney, also experienced unionists, were in agreement with the pro-CIO convention orientation. Of what importance could the evidence of the people be to Burnham, whose position derived from a syllogism of formal logic?

Having voted down the Field Committee's policy, the P.C. only then confronted its most disturbing problem. The meeting did not adjourn promptly as the sketchy minutes seem to indicate, but it continued for many hours after. The patently absurd "majority" that defeated Shachtman's motion (1 for, 2 against, 1 not voting, 1 abstaining), McKinney's motion (2 for, 2 against, 1 not voting) and carried Burnham's motion (3 for, 2 against) deprived the P.C. of the moral authority to enforce its position. L. . ., who had no vote, urged the comrades to give the Field Committee the right of way. Morrow, who continued to agree with Burnham's policy, joined L. . . in this proposal.

But those pleas fell on deaf ears. Shachtman did not come to their assistance. He failed to carry out his promise to the Field Committee, viz., in case of disagreement to publish a noncommittal news story in the *Socialist Appeal* until one or all of the field comrades could arrive in New York for further consultation. He failed to press the suggestion for a plenary session of the N.C., which was discarded by the meeting because it wasn't feasible and would take too long to convene. He betrayed the Field Committee and himself by merely giving lip-service to their position but capitulating under pressure to Burnham.

In fact, by this time he was already in a bloc with Burnham on the "organization" question: what were the formal powers of the P.C? With the question now turned upside down, and with McKinney, Abern, and Widick joining in the bloc, Burnham was in a position to crack his bureaucratic whip.

The only condition, Burnham threatened, whereby

the field could have precedence over the P.C. would be one in which he would resign from the committee. Abern immediately jumped into the breach: what an excellent opportunity for creating a party crisis! Yes, he too would resign, even though by his own admission it was a practical matter and the field might conceivably have its way. And Widick, brave Widick, he would likewise resign.

What a disgraceful exhibition!

In face of these threats the meeting adjourned sine die. The *Appeal* came off the press with the Burnhamistic pro-Martin convention policy smearing its front page.

Just reflect on this fateful incident for a minute:

A group of field workers, authorized by the Political Committee to direct a trade union campaign, adopts a policy on a practical trade union matter. Their position is concurred in by all the rank-and-file comrades directly engaged in the situation. The Political Committee, without consultation with these comrades, reverses their policy. It sends a competent reporter to the field who returns to New York in agreement with the Field Committee. The P.C. by a vote of 3 to 2, or 2 to 2 with 1 "not voting" rejects his report. The P.C. knows that every member of the National Committee, to which it is subordinated, who is cognizant of the situation favors the Field policy. In face of this crystal clear situation, the P.C. refuses to make any concession to the Field except on one condition: that Burnham, Abern, Widick, three of its leading members, resign. Intimidated by this threat, the P.C. decides to ram its unpopular policy down the throat of workers in the field.

If this isn't bureaucracy, what do you call it?

The act of resignation, under circumstances such as these, especially from leading committees of the party, is the hallmark of the petty bourgeois. The petty bourgeois cannot tolerate the idea of being in the minority. Thus during the auto crisis Burnham, Abern, and Widick were prepared to throw the party into crisis in order to avoid making a concession to the Field. Their split line today is only a logical culmination of their resignation line one year ago.

Not a word appears of this resignation in the "Bureaucratism" document, which succeeds in leaving the auto crisis untouched from Jan. 2 onward—when it really got under way! That's Burnham's conception of truth: don't print the news damaging to you.

V. THE 'SUPPRESSION' OF THE APPEAL

The same night, Thursday, January 26, Dunne, still in Detroit, received a long-distance call from Shachtman informing him of the slap in the face the P.C. had given the Field Committee. It is difficult to express our anger and resentment at the scandalous action of the Political Committee. We decided that Dunne was to leave for New York at the earliest possible moment for further consultation with the P.C. Far from defying the Political Committee, as minority slander has it, we were making every effort to arrive at an amicable agreement. Yet before Dunne could appear in New York to further persuade the committee, thousands of copies of the *Socialist Appeal* would arrive in Detroit, Flint, Toledo, and Cleveland. We were faced with a difficult, complicated problem.

It was, to be sure, our party duty to sell and distribute the official party organ. But we knew from experience, and later events confirmed our opinion, that the Burnham line would result in catastrophe for us as a similar line did for the Lovestoneites. We would make another attempt to convince the P.C. In the meantime we were determined that our work would not be jeopardized—the P.C. decision was, so to speak, not irrevocable. To prepare the comrades for the shock of the Burnhamistic *Appeal,* to soften the violent reaction on the part of the people who had yesterday been so enthusiastic and so unanimous for the Field Committee policy, comrades Cochran and Clarke went directly to the rank-and-file comrades in the four principal auto centers. We explained the situation in terms that were deliberately intended to preserve the prestige of the P.C. from the frightful damage it had inflicted upon itself. We were not entirely successful in this task, it is true—the bureaucratic methods of the committee stuck out like a sore thumb from our curtain of alibis and subterfuges. We urged the comrades not to distribute the *Appeal* and openly took the responsibility for this action on ourselves, pointing out how serious and extraordinary a measure this was!

But little urging was necessary. On the contrary, not a single copy of the *Socialist Appeal* would have been sold or distributed had we pounded the table, invoked the party constitution, and shouted ourselves hoarse. The program handed down to the rank-and-file workers violated their judgments and convictions to the utmost. They had a perfect right to ask that the distribution of that issue be held up until their complaints had been fairly heard.

This would seem an elementary axiom of party democracy. During the time of discussion, a minority is not coerced into carrying on public activity in behalf of the policy which it opposed. Following the discussion and decision, discipline applies universally to all. Those who do not accept the discipline either leave the party or are expelled from it. Not so for Burnham, however. For him there is a double standard: one for the leaders, one for the rank and file; one for the "intellectuals" and one for the workers. Thus Burnham lectured the Toledo, Cleveland, and Detroit branches in a letter signed by himself for the Political Committee:

"The only responsible way in which your branches could have proceeded would have been to distribute the *Appeal* in the usual manner and in the meanwhile to make known your protest and to attempt to secure a reversal of policy. From your point of view this would have meant trouble with respect to the workers in auto and perhaps elsewhere who would have been reached by those issues of the *Appeal*. But that temporary trouble, serious as it might have seemed or been, would not and does not compare to the trouble to the *party as a whole*, considered by the action you actually did take. We do not exaggerate when we say that your suppression of the *Appeal* has struck a heavy blow—not primarily at the P.C. as it might perhaps have seemed to you at the time—but at the entire party and its function. It will be some time before the party wholly recovers from this blow.

"We hope that these considerations will make clear to your branches the organizational attitude you adopted was impermissible, must be reversed, and ruled out for the future."

Notice the stiff, uncompromising tone of those paragraphs. They betray the man totally inexperienced with the workers' movement, where the official party paper has to be withheld from circulation many times for practical reasons or over disagreements with the center on tactics. Defeat the party in a class struggle action, compromise the rank-and-file workers in the eyes of their shopmates and fellow unionists—this the arrogant petty bourgeois can do without batting an eyelash. But never, never must you dare infringe on an arbitrary principle set up by the bureaucrat in his office.

We did not contest Burnham's letter in the field, although it alone might have set afoot a rank-and-file revolt the reverberations of which would have been buzzing to this day in the ears of Burnham and Company. We prevailed upon the branches to accept the letter of Burnham without protest, although the letter was a "heavy blow" directed mainly at us: we were concerned with upholding the prestige of the party leadership; we refused to allow the auto campaign to be detoured by Burnham's provocations.

How outrageous Burnham's letter actually was can be seen from one fact: *the policy of the P.C. was changed in favor of the Field Committee before this letter was written!*

How did the policy come to be changed?

VI. BURNHAM WASHES HIS HANDS OF THE 'DIRTY MESS'

On Monday, January 31, Comrade Dunne arrived in New York from Minneapolis. A meeting had been previously arranged for that afternoon. The meeting was called to order with a large group present. P.C. members: Shachtman, Abern, Widick, McKinney. N.C. members: V.R. Dunne, Morrow, L; N.C. alternates: Morgan, Erber, Milton. Comrades by invitation: Karsner, Stanley, Lebrun, Glenner. Cannon, who was in France, is recorded in the minutes as "(out of town)" and Gould as "(ill)."

Burnham appeared shortly after the meeting had been called to order and made the announcement that he would have to leave shortly for a dinner engagement and debate at the Labor Club of the ALP. Burnham could not be prevailed upon to break this engagement in favor of the extraordinary session of the Political Committee in progress. Dunne could manage to tear himself loose from the most vital activities of a labor movement affecting thousands of workers and travel 1,200 miles to discuss an important party problem. But Burnham could not break a dinner engagement of no importance to the party, the unions, or anyone else. By this procedure Burnham was making the supreme gesture of contempt, at which his class is so skillful. The patrician Burnham was allowing the plebeian Dunne to cool his heels as the price for questioning the higher authority. He would return at 10 p.m. after he had fulfilled his social obligations.

The meeting continued in a desultory fashion for hours. It was obvious to all that Burnham's deliberate absence was a demonstration of refusal to settle the crisis between the center and the field. How striking is the contrast between this haughtiness and arrogance and the considered efforts of Comrade Dunne to solve the crisis. To the petulant questions of these petty-bourgeois leaders who had lost in authority through no fault of their own, Dunne replied if he were presented with a choice—he would demand that the field carry out the line of the P.C. rather than see the resignation of leading P.C. members and the consequent precipitation of a deep-going party crisis.

Burnham did not return as he had promised at 10 p.m. The committee tentatively decided on proposals mutually agreeable but continued to burn the midnight oil for Burnham. No agreement was possible without his vote. Finally two hours later Burnham phoned and gave his assent to the following motions, which we summarize for lack of space:

1. A statement of policy on P.C.-Field Committee relations to be drafted and presented to the next P.C. meeting; 2. An article on the U.A.W. situation to be written by "Shachtman in line with proposals of the Auto-Sub Committee and in agreement with Dunne." 3. A motion by Shachtman on the proposal of Comrade Dunne that "a full meeting of the P.C. be held with the attendance of the leading comrades of the auto fraction" at the earliest possible time, date to be set at the convenience of the fraction.

Burnham however, had not yet written the final chapter to his role in the auto crisis. He had yet to write the statement where blame for the auto crisis was placed entirely at the door of the Field Committee, where the P.C. washed its hands of all responsibility for the policy it unanimously voted for at the January 31 meeting, where the field comrades were given a send-off in their work with prophecies of doom. At the February 7 meeting Burnham presented this statement. It was accepted unanimously. Shachtman and McKinney voted for it with a statement that their endorsement did not mean agreement with the "final paragraph because the inference may be drawn that my vote for it is at the same time an endorsement of the policy of the P.C. in the U.A.W. with which I do not agree." (Gould withheld his vote "until amply informed, in view of his absence from the meetings at which U.A.W. policy was discussed." Gould apparently was never "amply informed" as future meetings show no record of a vote by him on this subject.)

"The Statement of Policy in Auto" begins with a misrepresentation of the facts. It charges that responsibility for the disagreement rested with Cochran and Clarke with a confused policy: Clarke for boycott of both conventions, Cochran for attendance at both.

It denounces the comrades in the field for the "unprecedented step. . . . of suppressing the issue of the Appeal [containing the pro-Martin convention editorial—G.C.]. . . ." And further indicts the Field Committee by innuendo: "We do not wish herein to comment upon any questions of formal authority or discipline. . . ."

The statement washes its hands of all future responsibility for the work in auto: "Confronted with the facts the P.C. retained its conviction of the correctness of its point of view, and was thus confronted with the following condition. The attempt to carry out the policy of the P.C. majority (that is, the policy of the party) [With a stroke of a pen three members of the P.C, opposed by every informed N.C. member, trade unionist, and party auto worker, become the party!—G.C.] would be certain to lead to a major internal party crisis—quite apart from the specific effects on the work in auto; and, since there was and is no practical or technical means for the quick convening of a representative plenum of the N.C, there would be no way in which to solve the crisis."

The statement washes its hands of all future responsibility for the work in auto: "Confronted with the facts summarized above, the P.C. decided to put the direction of policy in auto for the next period—including what is presented in the party press—into the hands of the Auto Fraction and the N.C. field committee. The article appearing in the February 4th issue of the Appeal was prepared in accordance with this decision with the agreement of Comrade Dunne."

Finally, the prophecy of disaster: "The majority of the P.C. wishes it to be entirely clear that it holds to the point of view presented in the January 28th editorial and believes that the policy of the Fraction is seriously and dangerously wrong. It is convinced that the test of practice during the next weeks will make clear to the members of the Fraction their own error, and will demonstrate the correctness of the point of view of the P.C."

The P.C, according to this statement, did not make even the slightest error. The P.C. of Burnham, Widick, and Abern was the poor victim of the machinations of the rest of the party. Prestige politics, false pride, inability to admit error—these are mild characterizations of Burnham's statement.

Meanwhile the crisis simmered in the P.C. It was upset by the "broader internal problems which came to the surface in the dispute over policy in auto," so said the statement on Policy in Auto. And it continued: "The difficulty was aggravated by the unanimous opinion of the P.C. that the cleavage in this instance between the P.C. and the comrades concerned in the field was not the result merely of the differences of opinion in connection with the situation in auto but was related to other incidents during the past period." A dispute between Detroit and California over policy in the UAW further added to the consternation of the N.Y. committee.

On February 19, Smith, Dunne, and Goldman attended the meeting of the P.C. projected in the January 31 meeting. The meeting was not very fruitful. The main burden of complaint which ran through all the speeches of Shachtman, Burnham, Abern, and Widick can be summarized in a single sentence.

"It isn't so much that the field comrades opposed us. Rather, on the contrary this dispute would never have arisen if Cannon were here. They would never have dared challenge Cannon the way they did us."

Is it possible to answer such drivel? Can you prove to old ladies like these that Cannon's prestige derives from his deliberate aversion to such bureaucratic misuse of administration as Burnham-Shachtman were guilty of? Is it possible to convince such people by a citation from the record that Cannon always seeks out complete information before jumping to a policy, especially on trade union matters; that where there is disagreement on a practical matter where no political principle of the party program is involved between himself and field comrades he first of all attempts to persuade them that he is correct; that failing to persuade them—even though firmly convinced of the justice of his position—he yields in their favor? Can you explain to these people that this is an essential quality of leadership in a proletarian organization—in conjunction, of course, with a noteworthy record of being *correct* on practical matters of tactics? How can you convince people of such ABC propositions when their heads are full of "cliques," "plots," "machiavellian politics," and constant fear of the Stalinist degeneration of the future American Soviet through the mistakes of the Socialist Workers Party?

What could Goldman reply to Widick's whining that the field comrades had treated the P.C. with contempt, except to say that if it would satisfy Widick he would make a motion that the Field Committee do not treat them with contempt?

The minutes report "Agreement reached on carrying out the present auto policy. Unanimous agreement that suppression of *Appeal* by certain branches in the recent period was impermissible, and that such action is incompatible with the functioning of the party."

From a formal standpoint there could be no objections to the section of the motion concerning the *Appeal*. In reality, however, it was a deliberate and unjustified blow aimed by Burnham at the comrades in the field. The representatives of the Field Committee in New York were out of harmony with the spirit of this motion but they were first of all desirous of smoothing out the friction in the leading committee of the party. Their first aim was to create a condition in the party where its campaigns might be conducted without a continuing crisis. Moreover, they were confronted by an accomplished fact. Many days before this meeting, Burnham, in the name of the Political Committee, had mailed a letter of censure and condemnation to the Middle Western and California branches.

VII. CALIFORNIA INTERLUDE

The dispute in auto was further complicated by the situation in California. The comrades working in auto there were completely off the track. Through the activities of two or three comrades, not auto workers, they had established close relationships with Martin's machine in California, particularly

Los Angeles. They mistook the work they were doing for Irvan Carey, Martin's henchman, for a bloc. They were confused by the minutes of the National Auto Conference, calling for a Third Group but taking a noncommittal attitude on the two conventions. The P.C. raised a high wall between them and a correct policy. When in the next few days, the split in the UAW reached sharper proportions, David Stevens, L.A. organizer, wired Detroit and N.Y.: "Imperative we have policy in UAW. Wire whether we support Martin. Follow with detailed information. Reply very urgent." The date on the telegram (a similar one was received from Sam Myers in Oakland) is very important: January 28—that is, two days after the P.C. had rejected Comrade Shachtman's report and three days before it reversed itself in favor of the Field Committee under pressure of Comrade Dunne. Comrade Cochran wired back in agreement with Clarke that the policy was still under discussion but in the meantime he urged them to hold up distribution of the *Appeal.* (Unfortunately there is no copy of this telegram available in New York.) Widick, however, wired California in an entirely opposite sense: "Policy is to support Martin. It is contained in the January 28th edition of the *Appeal.* Copy of which being sent by airmail."

Widick's telegram was all the California comrades wanted. They immediately proceeded to distribute the January 28 edition of the *Appeal.* But they suppressed the next edition of the *Appeal,* which contained a change of line. It is monstrous for Burnham to shift responsibility onto the Field Committee for the failure of California to distribute the *Appeal.* They abstained from distribution for two reasons: 1. They were in favor of the January 28 line and opposed to the Field Committee because of their own erroneous policy. 2. They were confused and disoriented by the shifts in the P.C. position as reflected in the *Appeal.*

Instead of helping the California comrades correct their error—or turning that job over to the Field Committee entirely if the P.C. could not square this task with its conscience—Burnham wrote for the Political Committee a disloyal letter to the Los Angeles, East Oakland, and San Francisco branches. Under cover of a letter on the "suppression" of the *Appeal,* the following statements appear:

"We recognize especially the difficulties for the West Coast branches and what is in a sense the 'injustice' to these branches brought about through the fact that their representatives could not be present during the discussion leading to the new policy.

"We recognize also the right (and duty) of the West Coast branches to protest the new policy, if they do not agree with it, and to press through all *legitimate* means for a change. (We suggest that their point of view be made entirely clear to the N.C. field committee).

"We hope that these considerations will make it obvious to the California branches that the organizational attitude they have taken [suppressing the *Appeal*—G.C.] must be reversed. We say this naturally without in any way linking it to the matter of policy in auto—an issue which stands on its own merits—or with any intentions of denying the altogether just complaints about the manner in which the policy was arrived at."

Then follows a long confused paragraph about how the California comrades might build a third group and support neither convention and possibly even lean slightly in the direction of Martin.

This letter was sent two weeks after the P.C. had reversed its line, and one week after it had thrown all responsibility for the line on the Field Committee. The recitation of dates is comment enough.

But the letter of Burnham did not end the dispute with California. Burnham kept insisting in the P.C. meetings that the position of California supporting Martin supported his position. What sterile reasoning! Even if the California comrades were correct—and events proved them completely wrong—no national auto policy would be based on the situation in California. The central points of the auto industry, where automobiles are manufactured, are in Michigan, Ohio, and to a lesser extent Indiana. In those places too the UAW is strongest. To determine a policy on the basis of what was happening in California, the home of several auxiliary assembly plants and a few parts plants, is so obviously false as to require no answer.

But the California comrades were wrong even on the basis of the situation in their own state. The majority of the auto workers there—according to reliable reports which were available to the P.C. as well as the Field Committee and the California comrades—were for the Cleveland CIO convention and opposed to Martin. Our comrades there were prevented from acting upon these facts because of their disorientation by the Burnham Committee. The Field Committee had difficulty in correcting their error because of the complete lack of cooperation of the P.C., which refused to lend its support and authority to its efforts. It was not until Comrade Cannon arrived from France, months after the dispute with the P.C. had subsided, that California received its first letter from the P.C. indicating complete agreement with the Field Committee.

The comrades and the party in auto paid heavily for the bureaucratic attitude and the false policy of the P.C.

1. Burnham boasts that when he commits an error he is quick to admit it publicly. But the fact remains that the auto campaign received a severe blow from the inconsistency of the *Appeal,* which featured three different policies in three consecutive issues of the *Appeal.* Demagogues and Stalinists, who secured copies of the pro-Martin issue despite our careful concealment, exploited this inconsistency against us very effectively. The Lovestoneites had a Roman holiday over it in their "Workers Age."

2. It cost the party approximately $500 in train and plane fares alone to settle this dispute. This excludes long distance phone calls, telegrams, and large numbers of *Appeals* not distributed.

3. The work of the California comrades was completely disoriented.

VIII. THE QUESTION OF POLICY

The question of policy is a secondary consideration in a discussion of the party crisis over the auto situation. That is why we have reserved it for last place. Any person, any leader of the party, is liable to make a mistake on a matter of practical policy, particularly on a trade union question. As a matter of fact such mistakes are made quite frequently, and only a fool would condemn a leader for this or that incidental mistake. Yet Burnham's "mistake" on the auto situation is on the same order of his "mistake" on the Russian question. His empirical, formalistic, nondialectical method of thinking is revealed in the auto question no less than it is in the Russian question.

To understand the auto situation and party policy in it, it is necessary to go back to the convention of the UAW in Milwaukee in August 1937.

Martin was confronted at that convention with a powerful opposition representing almost 50 percent of the convention delegates, known as the "Unity Group." This opposition was led in part by the Stalinists, it is true, but the Stalinists were exploiting through the "Unity Group" the most militant and democratic sentiments of the best rank-and-file progressives. The worker militants were jealous of their democratic rights and for a militant union. Martin was abusing these democratic rights and attempting to "stabilize" the union. The revolt against him was entirely healthy even though it was misdirected by the Stalinists. Supporting Martin at that convention were the worst type of office-holders and the most reactionary and backward members of the union.

We gave the Unity Group critical support at that convention, attempting in the meanwhile to organize an uprising within it against the Stalinists. Following the convention we made several attempts to organize an independent group which would oppose Martin and at the same time fight the Stalinists, who were not interested in a struggle against the bureaucracy but were rather seeking a deal with the administration. Unfortunately, our weakness condemned this effort to failure.

In the Spring of the following year, 1938, events took a new turn in the auto union. The Stalinists had pried Frankensteen, Martin's chief lieutenant, away from him, and were now making an open bid for power—against the wishes of their allies, the SP group led by Reuther and Mazey, who headed powerful locals in the auto union. It was now, for the first time, possible to conduct an open struggle against the Stalinists which the workers would understand. Seeing our opportunity we sent a delegation to Martin which was successful in persuading him to adopt the program we presented (later revised by him and popularly known in the UAW as the 20-point program). With this program Martin pledged to take positive action in the pressing organizational problems that confronted the union, to guarantee the locals their autonomy and rank and file democracy, and to conduct a militant fight against the corporations. And also to fight the Stalinist "collective security" propaganda with an antiwar campaign.

The program met with instantaneous success. It is not an exaggeration to say that it swept the union with the power of a new dispensation. The Stalinists were completely stymied. Unfortunately, Martin was not the man to carry the program through to the end. No sooner were the Stalinists defeated at the Executive Board than Martin entrusted the union administration to some of his incompetent lieutenants and boarded his plane to make speeches at banquets and meetings where everything was discussed but the auto workers' problems and everybody was present but the auto workers. Within a month, the Stalinists attempted to usurp power. Instead of going to the rank and file and crucifying the Stalinists ideologically as we had urged him, Martin expelled five of them from the Executive Board. From that time on Martin behaved like an hysterical old lady, revoking local chapters, appointing administrators over locals, and allying himself with the worst reactionaries. Within three months Martin had completely nullified the effectiveness of the 20-point program and antagonized that section of the rank and file which had begun to move in his direction. Once again he was isolated and the Stalinists had begun to recoup their former power as the self-appointed champions of democracy.

From that time on we began to steer a course away from Martin. Through the months of September, October, November, and December 1938 our criticism of Martin constantly sharpened in its tone. We had felt Martin's reactionary policies personally. Bert Cochran, appointed by Martin at the time of the adoption of the 20-point program as Detroit UAW-WPA director, was summarily removed from office. The McCord strike, led by our comrades, was betrayed by one of Martin's lieutenants without Martin lifting a finger. In the month of December our criticism of Martin had become condemnation. At a meeting of the National Auto Fraction held on December 25, 1938—minutes of which were mailed into the National Office—Cochran reported as follows:

"Our line in auto is changed today, the orientation being against the administration of the UAW. Our aim today is that of building a new progressive group with the objective that this group may win the leadership of the union—Our general aim is the creation of a new group in auto. We can only agitate for it and present our program. Later, when our forces grow we may find allies in the S.P. in Detroit, groups in the West Side Local and Briggs local who were part of the Unity Group—and organize a loose alliance with them for a progressive group on the basis of our program."

It is alleged by the Opposition that the auto policy—ostensibly a pro-Martin policy—was decided at the January 1 meeting. This is absurd. It was evident to all present that the situation was in the process of change while we were meeting and no definitive policy could be formulated from the distance of New York. The question of policy was left undecided at the meeting, and no policy motion was recorded at the P.C. meeting on January 3.

If there had been a pro-Martin policy adopted at that meeting, how explain the article Cochran wrote for the January 21 issue of the *Appeal*, entitled "Faction Fight Flares Again in U.A.W. Executive Board"? It characterized the two groups ("the Martin and Mortimer crowd") as gangs whose scandals had exhausted the patience of the membership. It referred to the "record of stewardship of the International Executive Board and the International Officers" as one of "opportunism, stupidity, supineness, treachery." It called upon "the automobile workers to turn thumbs down on fake leaders whether of the Peiper-Hauser type or job-holders of the Mortimer-Stalinist type of bureaucrats. . . ."

When the Field Committee adopted its original program under the title: "One Convention—One Union—One Fight Against the Employers" it had these salient facts in mind: Martin was thoroughly discredited by his reactionary and bureaucratic policies, the Ford scandal unscrupulously exploited by the Stalinists only adding to his discreditment. Only the most conservative and backward workers supported him. The Stalinists were growing in disfavor with the auto workers because of their vicious, unprincipled factionalism. The Stalinists could now pose as champions of democracy only with the greatest of difficulty after they had brought in and saddled upon the union the CIO receivership of Hillman-Murray. The Reuther-Mazey-Marshall (Chrysler local president) group had already broken with the Stalinists. The workers were nauseated with the internecine struggle and were seeking a road to unity and struggle against the corporations.

Our line was, in the colloquial expression, "a natural." It denounced both groups on the Executive Board of the union for bankruptcy in organization, bureaucracy in internal affairs, capitulation before the corporations, and for leading the union to the brink of a split. It called for unity of the union against both groups on the basis of a nine-point "Union Building Program." The program found an immediate and welcome response among wide layers of the auto workers union. The Detroit newspapers understood the significance of the "Third Group" and gave it leading publicity. At the Cleveland convention many of the planks of the program were adopted with great enthusiasm.

We can confidently assert that had Martin not split from the CIO, the original "Third Group" program would have catapulted our small group into a position of great influence and strength. But when Martin bolted the CIO, the situation changed almost overnight. The workers know that Martin was moving towards the AFL, which they despised almost as much as the corporations, and they began to line up. In a short while the overwhelming bulk of militant workers had taken their place in the anti-Martin, pro-CIO camp. The Stalinists could stage another comeback by shouting their patriotism to the CIO. With the most militant workers determined first of all to defeat Martin and the AFL, our small third group could at best play a modest role at the Cleveland convention.

Burnham charged in his Statement on Policy in Auto that Clarke was originally in favor of boycotting both conventions, and Cochran of participating in both conventions. In his answer to Trotsky he charges that both Cochran and Clarke were in favor of boycotting both conventions. His charge is false in both instances. They arise out of Shachtman's report, in which Shachtman completely misunderstood what Cochran and Clarke stated to him in response to his demand for a "concrete answer." The situation was still too unclear, too fluid, and too turbulent to require an immediate answer to the question of "which convention?" Our policy was best served at this juncture by concentrating on the slogan unity of the UAW against both groups on the basis of a positive program. The phrase "a plague on both your houses" was used to epitomize this policy and referred specifically not to the conventions but to the Stalinist and Martin group. The easy transition we made between this policy and the pro-CIO policy proves that far from playing "abstentionist" politics, we had set a general line in a complicated situation and were waiting for events to indicate what the next practical step would be.

Burnham boasts in his answer to Trotsky that contrary to Clarke and Cochran's *abstentionism* in auto he formulated a concrete policy. How did he formulate this "concrete" policy, by what process of thought? What would have been the results of his policy had it been carried out?

You will recall in the quotation cited from his editorial in the January 28 edition of the *Appeal* his statement that the "Cleveland meeting will be a 100% Stalinist stooge assembly."

He continued: "Every move, every motion, every resolution will be dictated by Earl Browder in exactly the same manner that he dictates the proceedings of the American League for Peace and Democracy, the I.W.O., or the conventions of the Communist Party itself. The future of the union movement in auto does not and cannot lie with the Cleveland puppet-show. . . . The locals must elect their delegates to the Detroit convention, not to submit to Martin but to re-establish the rule of the members over their own union."

Here are the full blossoms of Burnham's undialectical thinking:

"The Stalinists . . . for their own counterrevolutionary pro-war political ends. . . ." "Everything healthy in the labor movement withers under the touch of Stalinism." (From the same editorial).

What follows from this: The Cleveland convention "will be a 100% Stalinist stooge assembly." Its every "move" will be dictated by Browder in the same manner he dictates to the I.W.O. or to the C.P. itself.

And further: "The future of the union movement in auto does not and cannot lie with the Cleveland puppet-show."

Or: Martin is "also responsible for the disaster." His policies have been "reactionary." He has played into the "hands of the Stalinists."

But Martin is opposed to the Stalinists, who are "a counterrevolutionary and pro-war" political force under whose touch "everything healthy in the labor movement withers."

Therefore support Martin's convention—"not to submit" to Martin, of course, but to "re-establish the rule of the members over their own unions."

The formal logic here is perfect. But just one little thing is omitted from this syllogism, just as it is omitted from all formal logic: an understanding of events in the process of motion and change, an understanding of the interaction of human beings and events. Or in other words, an understanding of the dynamics of the workers' movement.

It is true that the Stalinists represented a patriotic, counterrevolutionary political force. But large masses of auto workers followed them, not for that reason but because the Stalinists posed as progressives, militants, and union democrats.

It is true that the Stalinists would play a leading role at the Cleveland convention. But the great masses of auto workers would go to Cleveland not for that reason but because they had confidence in the CIO as a progressive, healthy force in the labor movement, and because they were bitterly opposed—and justifiably so—to the AFL.

It is true that the Stalinists would play a leading role in Cleveland. But that did not mean that Earl Browder would dominate it like he does a convention of the I.W.O. or the C.P. To say that is not to understand the difference between a political party and a trade union. To say that is to be completely ignorant of or completely ignore the great democratic, rank-and-file tradition of the turbulent auto workers movement. To say that is to completely underestimate the role of John L. Lewis or Sidney Hillman, who, for good bureaucratic reasons, would not tolerate such an arrangement for one minute in a union where they had any voice or influence at all.

It is true that Martin was opposed to the Stalinists. But how had he opposed the Stalinists? As a reactionary, not as a progressive. Who would be most likely to follow Martin? Certainly not the militant workers, whom he had done everything in his power to alienate and drive away. Who would go to Detroit, which was oriented towards the AFL? Only the backward, the privileged or conservative workers who looked upon the CIO as a "Red" organization, always creating trouble for the employer in the plants—workers seeking the road of class collaboration. In truth, to go to this convention "not to submit to Martin" but to "re-establish the rule of the rank and file" would be like going to a Communist Party convention (all proportions guarded) "not to submit" to Stalin or Browder but to re-establish the rule of the rank and file.

Burnham's undialectical thought on this question is of a piece with his undialectical thinking on the Russian question. The Soviet Union is dominated by counterrevolutionary, Bonapartist, Stalinist bureaucrats. These bureaucrats are the worst enemies of the Soviet and international working class. Therefore, be for the defeat of the Soviet Union in the war.

Or: the workers' state is a democratic structure which improves the standard of living of the workers. In the Soviet Union totalitarianism has replaced democracy and the standard of living has improved only in favor of the bureaucrats. Therefore, the Soviet Union is not a workers' state; it is a Stalinist bureaucratic state.

Burnham is proud of his undialectical method of thought. He says it enables him to predict—indeed only on that basis is any method of thought efficacious. On February 7 Burnham made a prediction in the Statement on Policy in Auto, endorsed by Widick and Abern:

"The majority of the P.C. wishes it to be entirely clear that it holds to the point of view presented in the January 28th editorial [the one cited immediately above—G.C.] and believes that the policy of the Fraction is seriously and dangerously wrong. It is convinced that the test of practise during the next weeks will make it clear to the members of the Fraction their own error, and will demonstrate the correctness of the point of view of the P.C."

If ever a prediction was knocked into a cocked hat it was this one.

The Cleveland convention of the UAW represented the great majority of auto workers from all the important corporations—Chrysler, General Motors, Briggs Body, Studebaker, Hudson, Wyllis, etc., etc., from all the important centers of Michigan, Ohio, Indiana, and Wisconsin. Far from the convention being a Stalinist stooge convention, a powerful opposition functioned against the Stalinists from the day the convention opened. One of the largest locals in the union openly sported "brooms" as their emblem of a campaign to sweep out the former Executive Board. At least half of the points in our program were taken up by other delegates and pushed through the convention. Far from Browder dictating the decisions of the convention, the Stalinists had to fight for every position tooth and nail. There was no red-baiting at Cleveland. And as to the future of this convention, the UAW-CIO regained nearly all of the members it had lost to Martin, defeated him decisively in every NLRB election; it has signed contracts with every major auto corporation with the exception of Ford.

On the other hand Martin's convention was a complete fiasco. Its delegates came almost exclusively from small shops, representing small groups of workers in out-of-the-way cities. The delegates from the large locals were completely trumped up and represented no one but themselves. The composition of the convention was backward and conservative, and nine-tenths of the proceedings were devoted to problems entirely extraneous to the real problems of unionism.

They were against the "radicalism," the "communism," and "trouble-making" of the CIO. The sessions were devoted to flag-waving patriotism and rabid red-baiting. The convention was a Martin stooge assembly—eulogies of Martin were as regular, frequent, and repulsive as they are in a C.P. convention—because without Martin the convention was without leader or reason for existence. The Lovestoneites, forced into a corner like rats by the right wing around Martin, were compelled to put up the semblance of an opposition. They tried "not to submit"—but came to the most ignominious end. This convention marked the public suicide of the Lovestoneites in auto just as it would have marked our own had we participated in it.

A party comrade came to this convention from California—not as the delegate of his local but as the representative of a minority. His hotel room was constantly infested with reactionaries who ranted from early morning to late at night against "reds," "Lovestoneites," "Trotskyites"; his movements were watched by them and he was shadowed through the streets; he met with the auto committee of the party only in greatest secrecy; he did not dare take the floor at the convention; he was almost expelled both by the rump Martin group and by the controlling CIO local when he returned to Los Angeles.

As to Martin's future: his locals left him one by one until he was left with only a shell. He practiced strikebreaking in the CIO strikes in GM and Briggs. He united with Gerald Smith and Coughlin against the CIO in the Chrysler lockout. He is the most discredited man in the auto union.

Now, for the first time in a year, Burnham publicly admitted his mistake—and only with a hateful snarl at those who corrected him—and we were supposed to see and admit our error in "the next weeks"! Need more be said?

The picture of the leadership of the petty-bourgeois opposition as it would look at the helm of our party or at the helm of its own group if their threat of split is carried out, can be drawn from the highly symptomatic events of the auto crisis:

Burnham: revealed strong tendencies towards bureaucratism in administration, an arrogant approach to the rank and file, a hateful attitude towards the workers who correct his line, sterile and formalist in analysis. By his own admission, he is an undialectical thinker. (See "Science and Style.")

Shachtman: revealed an indecisiveness in position, a Hamlet-like attitude under pressure, which made him a tool of the strongest force and treacherous to the political convictions of his fellow-thinkers and of himself. In the auto crisis Shachtman demonstrated symptoms of this disease, observed many times in him prior to and subsequent to these events.

As for Abern, Trotsky's characterization of him needs no improvement: "Abern long ago came to the conclusion that Marxism [and even concrete policy on practical matters as the auto crisis proved—G.C.] is a doctrine to be honored but a good oppositional combination is something far more substantial."

IX. EPILOGUE ON A SLANDER

To cover up their bureaucratic methods and false policy, the Opposition whispers: anyway nothing was achieved in auto; the campaign was a flop. They do not dare say this out loud because they know—or do they?—that policies and methods are not judged by immediate results to the party.

Concrete conditions have at least as much to do with results as do party energy and party policy.

Still they slander the campaign and its achievements.

We were confronted with big obstacles in our drive in auto. Early in the campaign accidental circumstances entirely beyond our control completely prevented us from utilizing our new contacts as we had planned to on January 1. The turn in events in the auto union did not help our small group break out of its isolation. The lack of important locals or prominent spokesmen prevented us from playing an outstanding role at the UAW convention.

Yet despite these obstacles we rolled up solid achievements, modest though they were, for the party. Our program and group was respected and popular among the militants. Many sections of it were adopted at the convention. We had a caucus of fifteen delegates in Cleveland, in contrast to two at Milwaukee, the previous convention of the union. Through our program and activities at the convention we made contacts in many cities and among auto worker militants where we had none before.

The *Socialist Appeal,* through widespread distribution, became the most widely read radical paper in the auto union. This was the principal work of our untiring Detroit comrades, whose lack of growth is attributable to factors far beyond the control of the campaign or the party. Only now Detroit is making its first real gains in recruitment of auto unionists.

The Flint Branch blossomed forth as a genuine proletarian branch with solid auto worker composition, leading influence in the CIO-WPA local, and tremendous possibilities in the main auto workers local of the city. This was our greatest achievement.

TOWARD THE PARTY CONVENTION

by James P. Cannon

I. BEFORE THE NATIONAL PARTY CONVENTION

June 13, 1939

All attention of the revolutionary militants in the United States is now turned toward the antiwar convention of the Socialist Workers Party, which is to convene in New York City on July 1. Without doubt this assembly will mark an important stage in the development of the only serious, the only genuine opposition to the impending war.

It is not to be expected, however, that the convention will produce any new prescription or panacea. Those who look for miracles will be disappointed. We do not conceive of the struggle against war as some sort of special task, separated from the struggle against the capitalism which breeds it. Antiwar sentiments, as such and in themselves, mean nothing; everybody, more or less, is against war. Opposition to war that aims at social revolution—that alone is significant. And that, in turn, is totally merged with the struggle to build a revolutionary party, which points the way, and to connect it with the masses of workers who have the power.

A convention—any convention—is not an all-saving instrument; its potentialities are strictly limited. It can sum up the past but it cannot assure the future. It cannot change anything in the status of the party which exists on the day it convenes. It can at best only estimate what is valuable in the work of the past, what has been achieved and must be firmly retained as well as what must be rejected. The future tasks can be indicated by the convention, but their accomplishment—or their default—will rest with the party after the convention adjourns its sessions. Even so, conventions are large and irreplaceable experiences in the life of every democratic, that is, every real, party.

Estimating Our Past

The forthcoming antiwar convention of the American Section of the Fourth International will enable us to pause and look collectively in two directions—at the past and at the future. Our survey of the past can only assure us that our preliminary work is done, and, for the most part, not badly. We have built firmly, our achievements have a mighty historic significance. This we know and nobody can tell us differently. Our program has withstood all the tests of theory and experience, and stands unassailable. We have assembled the forces of the vanguard in a single organization. We no longer have any rivals in this field, and no problems of "unity" require a second thought. The ten years' task of clearing the air of confusion and programmatic disorientation, of regrouping the scattered forces of the revolutionary fighters under a new, clean banner; the same work which occupied so many of the years of the time of Marx, and after him of Lenin, is already behind us. Indeed, the hour for our full concentration on broader tasks struck some time ago.

The Root of All Our Evil

Our sluggishness in making the abrupt turn to mass work with all force and energy; the persistence of old habits of our days of isolation as a propaganda circle; our failure to reach new, fresh strata of workers; our hesitation, half-hearted, at the brink of the great stream represented by the workers' mass movement;—herein is the root of all our evil. The convention must take sober account of these facts and say something decisive about them. With the tasks of yesterday accomplished and those of today only half understood and appreciated in a gingerly way, we are marking time while the forces of reaction, which already outline the features of an authentic American fascism, grow by leaps and bounds. The position is becoming dangerous. The convention, true enough, cannot rectify matters, but it can and must sound the alarm and summon the party to rigorous measures for a speedy rectification in the coming months. Time, as the legal maxim has it, is of the essence of the contract. There is not too much time, even in America.

We can make up for lost time and begin to forge ahead if we turn our faces in the right direction. That means, first of all, to turn our backs on the pessimists and the calamity-howlers, the soul-sick intellectuals and tired radicals who whine and dawdle around the fringes of the movement and even, to a certain extent, infest its ranks. These gentry, whose gaze is concentrated on their own navels, do not see what is going on about them. It is a simple fact that American capitalism, the most powerful of all, is already seized by paralyzing senility. It writhes in an ever-deepening social crisis which its most perspicacious politicians no longer hope to cure but only to alleviate, and that only by desperate gamble of war. It is a fact that the furious onslaughts against the workers, employed and unemployed, signalize in essence the acknowledgment that the over-rich American capitalism can no longer pretend to assure a living to the slave within his slavery. It is a fact that the sum total of all these circumstances—is rapidly preparing all the preconditions of a social revolution. And confronting it is the working class that has not known defeat, that has invincible numbers and boundless power.

All this is a sealed book to those skeptics, who in general, have thought very little about the scientific analysis of capitalism upon which revolutionary calculations are predicated, and still less about the laboring masses as the all-powerful makers of revolution. Their melancholy sentiments have no relation to the actual situation in this country. They attempt to record the status and the prospects of the revolutionary movement by the fluctuating fever chart of their own unstable moods. They are mistaken; and doubly mistaken are those militants who even for a moment heed these counsels of petty-bourgeois impotence and despair.

The pessimistic brotherhood comprises several categories, loosely united by a common bond of despair, who carry on like keeners at a wake. Some of them, the well-known tired radicals, are like "gymnasium fighters" who exhaust all their strength in training and enter the real battle in the ring beaten and ready to quit before they start. Others have looked so often for the revolution before it was due and were so often disappointed that they can't recognize it when it finally approaches. Others, and they are not numerically the least, are simply afraid of the shadow of war and fascism, and flee the battle before it really begins.

Most contemptible of all are those who seek to cover their desertion and retreat by hurling newly invented "ideological" disagreements with Marxism over their shoulders. Taken all together they are an unattractive and uninspiring aggregation. It is nothing less than a monstrous travesty to consider them as in any way reflecting the movement of workers' emancipation which, by its very nature, is alien to all pessimism and defeatist sentiments. It is criminal folly to waste time or even to argue the question with these runaway-boys and heralds of defeat before the battle.

Turn to the Source of Power

Our convention must let the dead bury the dead and turn the face of the party to the workers, who are the real source of power and of inspiration and well-grounded optimism. We *had* said this before. More than once we have incorporated it in resolutions. But we have not made the turn in forthright fashion. That is why we are lagging behind. That is the main reason we are suffering a certain stagnation. That is why we are even flirting with the danger of a degeneration of the party along the lines of conservative passivity, introspection, and futility.

The proletariat of the United States is the source of unlimited power. It can raise the whole world on its shoulders—that is the unshakeable premise of all our calculations and all our work. "But what," say the croakers—pointing to the heavy defeats in Europe—"what if France and all Europe goes down before fascism?" We answer: The issue in France is not decided yet, but even in the worst case, the workers of America have power enough to topple over the structure of capitalism and to lift the whole world with them when they rise!

The foundation convention of the party a year and a half ago gave us pretty clear directives regarding orientation to the workers' mass movement. The revolutionary transition program has equipped us with the necessary slogans and proposals for effective agitation on the realities of the day. We made some progress, but all too little do we consider the breathtaking speed at which the social crisis is developing. The fault for that is not in the objective circumstances—they are favorable enough—nor in our stars, but in ourselves. We have not yet grown up to the level of our gigantic tasks.

We made some headway while other parties making pretensions to radicalism were slipping backward. We held our cadres intact while others suffered disintegration. We sloughed off quite a few crack-pots, and that is an advantage not to be discounted. By dint of considerable effort and sacrifice, we established the twice-weekly *Appeal.* But all this weighs too little in the scale against the mushroom emergence of fascist movements and the sweeping growth in the influence of fascist demagogy. There are our rivals in the struggle for power. Comparison with them is the real criterion by which we must estimate our own achievements. And that criterion tells us warningly: Slow, modest, steady growth will not avail. We must leap ahead.

For us there is no way but forward at an accelerated pace. Can we solve the financial crisis of our twice-a-week *Appeal* by means of expansion? Can we strengthen and improve our responsibility, our discipline, and our morale? Can we blast a path to fresh circles of undefeated and undiscouraged workers, and make our party in truth a party of the proletariat in its composition and in all of its activity?

Affirmative answers to these questions and concrete, practical plans to implement them, are what the party needs from the convention.

II. BLAST A WAY FORWARD WITH A PROGRAM OF PARTY EXPANSION

June 16, 1939

The question of war, which leads directly to the question of revolution, confronts every workers' political organization with its supreme test. It is as clear as day and nobody any longer denies that capitalism, which has overstayed its time as a social and economic system, is about to inflict upon humanity another worldwide military explosion.

It is self-evident that America, the greatest and most rapacious imperialist power, will be directly involved in the war, as it is already involved in the diplomatic maneuvers which precede and prepare it. Irreconcilable opposition to the war is the prerequisite for the development of a revolutionary struggle to end the war with a workers' victory. As the only party in the United States whose opposition to war is taken seriously either by itself or others, we have to consider now the practical ways and means to make our opposition effective and emerge from the revolutionary crisis, which will inevitably ensue from the war, at the head of the revolting masses. This question will of necessity dominate our forthcoming antiwar convention from beginning to end.

But what does it mean to begin now to prepare an effective opposition to the war? Obviously it cannot be done by a passive waiting for war to break out. On the contrary it means to gear up all our work to a speed and intensity which breaks completely with the snail's pace movement of "normal" and peaceful times. That is the gist of our problem. Unless we solve it we are lost. The trouble with us, the mortal danger that confronts us, is that our revolutionary antiwar program may remain on paper. We have repeated again and again that the fight against war is not a special task to be accomplished by some sort of sleight-of-hand. If war is only the continuation of politics by other means, then the revolutionary struggle against war is the multiplied extension and intensification of revolutionary agitation and organization. We must prepare for war by building a stronger party and reshaping it for war conditions. And we must make haste and perform miracles of energy in the time left to us.

Old Methods Outmoded

The social crisis of capitalism is unfolding at such hurricane speed, with a world war on the order of the day, that the slow, modest growth of past times, the patient enrollment and education of new recruits, one by one—the only thing possible in our preparatory years—is fatally inadequate now. We must drive ahead: everything must be done in a hurry and on a many times multiplied scale.

Fortunately, we are ready for such a radical transformation of the nature of our work and activity. In cooperation with our co-workers of the Fourth International we have worked out the program. We have educated cadres who constitute the skeleton of a national organization. We are ready, prepared by the past, to drive forward and become a proletarian power if we have the will to do so.

This we can do without undue strain. In our ranks we have great reservoirs of untapped energy. We are not tired: nobody in our organization has hurt himself very much yet. True, our militants have done much more than others, and have made sacrifices which astound the other parties of half-and-half policies and half-and-half people. But we are not like the others; we aim to conquer the world. We need to put the party now on a war footing and move ahead by a forced march. We need to break with the habits of conservative routine and blast our way out of isolation by a bold and ambitious program of expansion.

'Moral Re-armament'

Our antiwar convention must give the signal for a "moral re-armament" of our own, in the sense of transforming our more or less placid, easy-going propaganda circle into an army on the march; an army whose disciplined militants are determined to conquer and shrink back from no endeavor and no sacrifice. We must aspire to build such a party as Lenin built, and to adapt to the conditions of America his concept of professional revolutionists, who live and work all the time for the party and with the party. The convention, in calling for such a transformation, should implement it by setting concrete tasks which, by their very nature, will operate to hasten the process.

Up till now, for explainable reasons, we have been a party primarily of literary propagandists and critics. On the organization side we have been woefully weak, and we have made only a few feeble experiments with mass organization. This lopsidedness, which had its justification in our days of preparation, must be corrected now by a drastic shift in emphasis. Propaganda, which Plekhanov defined as the dissemination of many ideas to a few people, must be counterbalanced by a ten-fold increase in agitation work, which he defined as the spreading of a few ideas to many people. That is the true meaning of our transitional program. To accomplish this in a few months' time—that is all we can allow for the change—we need a concrete program of expansion as follows.

The Three-a-Week Appeal

1. On the literary front: Change the *Appeal* to a more popular paper and publish it three times a week as the necessary next step on the road to the daily *Appeal.*

2. On the organization front: Draft twenty more qualified comrades to work at full time for the party. One each should specialize in and direct Trade union, unemployed, and Negro work on a national scale. The others should be assigned to work in the field—at least one full-time organizer in every important district or center where we have party organizations and a few men roaming the field to organize new branches and develop new activities.

3. Agitation: Regular speaking tours for party leaders at intervals of not more than two months.

4. Finances: Raise a special fund of $10,000 to finance the foregoing undertakings.

This program, so modest in comparison with the magnitude of our tasks and the limited time at our disposal, is of course only a beginning. But once it is fairly in operation it will produce the new means and possibilities for further expansion. It should be realized within a period of three or four months after the convention.

There is no doubt whatever that we can realize the program in full without any real strain on our resources and energies of our members and sympathizers. To be sure, any other party of comparative size would be flabbergasted by half these demands. But again—we are not like the others. We set ourselves tasks which are in some degree commensurate with our great aims and the quality of our militants. The demands of this expansion program will appear as child's play compared to the real tasks and sacrifices which are yet to come, and for which the minor efforts and sacrifices of the expansion program will help to prepare us.

Our convention, I venture to say, will not stutter over the sacrifices this program entails; more likely it will ask proof of its practical feasibility.

From this standpoint I will discuss the question here briefly.

Isn't it foolhardy to undertake a three-a-week publication when the two-a-week is admittedly in serious financial difficulties which, only a few weeks ago, threatened its suspension? No, it is not foolhardy, but on the contrary is entirely feasible. We need the paper three times a week in order to get ready for the Daily which will be on the agenda tomorrow.

The twice-a-week *Appeal* is already four months old. It is an inestimable weapon, as all recognize. We strike now twice as hard and twice as often and we distribute approximately twice as many papers as before. The only trouble is a very small one. Naturally, we operate on a close margin. Some of the branches became careless in the payment of their bundle order accounts. Quite a few have been too sluggish in getting subscriptions. Remedy these defects—and the convention, by its authority, undoubtedly can and will remedy them; put a stop to horse-play about the payments for bundle orders; and increase the subscription list by only 1,000 by the mandatory assignment of quotas; and the twice-a-week *Appeal* will be financially stabilized. The decks cleared for the next necessary step—the three-a-week *Appeal.*

Half for Organization Work

We will, of course, require a reserve fund to cover the deficit and help the paper over the first period. One half of the $10,000 fund should be allocated to this purpose. The other half should be spent exclusively on organization work as outlined above.

Ten thousand dollars is quite a sum of money for a small organization of poor people to raise at one time. But the rank and file of our organization have shown in the past that they are capable of responding with enthusiasm and sacrifice every time real needs and serious tasks are presented to them in a rational fashion. The 100 percent achievement of the quotas for the twice-a-week *Appeal* and the simultaneous collection of the international fund should be eye-openers to those who doubt that our militants are ready to take a step forward and to pay for it, if necessary, with their own skin.

The whole party is dissatisfied, and properly so, with the way our organization work lags behind the literary propaganda. Part of the difficulty can be attributed to individual delinquencies which may or may not be corrected in the coming months. But a convention discussion on this level and a chorus of recrimination cannot yield anything very valuable. That would be simply nibbling at the problem, anyway. We need not merely an adjustment here and there—although that will be useful—but a drastic, wholesale reconstruction of our conceptions and methods of organization. We must have done with amateurism and the lackadaisical organizing methods of a propaganda sect that does not contemplate big actions. We need a bigger staff, not only in the center but also, and especially, in the field.

We have the qualified people to make up such a staff, young militants who have received their political education in our incomparable school, who balk at no sacrifice and are ready for any assignment. At the same time the party has reached the point where it needs and must have their undivided labors. The three-a-week *Appeal* and the augmented staff of organizers can soon lift the party higher and prepare it better for bigger things to come.

The convention will mark a real step forward if it adopts a program of expansion along these lines.

III. NEW DIRECTIONS REQUIRE NEW METHODS OF PARTY WORK

June 20, 1939

A revolutionary party begins with an idea, and the idea—that is, the program—becomes an all-conquering power capable of transforming society when it permeates the mass. The work of attracting the masses to the revolutionary program does not proceed along a straight line by the simple repetition of propaganda. If that were so, working class politicians would not be necessary. A good phonograph—or a sectarian, which is the same thing—would suffice. The struggle for the support of the majority of the working class, the prerequisite for the socialist victory, is an extremely complicated struggle, and one which, moreover, is constantly changing and constantly imposing shifts in emphasis and different methods of work. It is necessary to keep a clear view of the goal, but that alone is not enough. The art of revolutionary politics consists in recognizing the most favorable immediate objective and of concentrating, according to the military motto, all forces on the point of attack. Only thus is it possible to move forward.

Lenin spoke of the necessity of seizing the right link in the chain. And Trotsky crammed all practical political wisdom into a single sentence when he said the most important of all questions is, what to do next. The tactical orientation of the moment depends on what is necessary and what is possible at the moment.

The Way Is Cleared

Our goal is and has been always the same—the winning over of the masses for the revolutionary struggle for power. It was the same in our formative years when we disregarded the "mass work" windbags, as later when we turned to broader fields of political activity and broke with the sectarians. If we say today, with at least the formal agreement of the whole party, that our work must now be concentrated directly on mass work, it is because the road has been cleared for such a turn. The rather sad fact that our practices in this respect have by no means caught up with our resolutions does not signify any intention on our part to deceive ourselves by our unanimous declarations. We mean what we say and will learn how to act accordingly.

Nobody at the convention will argue against the necessity of a full concentration on mass work. Nobody will propose that we go back and chew the fat once again with the sectarian cliques who have theorized themselves into a secluded corner and remain there to everybody's satisfaction—their own and ours and that of the world at large. It is unimaginable that anyone should suggest that we go back and fight over again the factional struggle within a common organization with the Thomasite "socialists." That chapter is finished. What was once alive and revolutionary there belongs now to the American section of the Fourth International.

As for the spurious "unity" campaign of the Lovestoneites—is it possible that any member of our party can be caught on this hook? Hardly. This petty stratagem of the Lovestoneite leadership—as transparently crooked as its authors—is designed only as artificial stimulation for a doomed and dwindling sect without program or prospects or good repute, and a cover-up for the real object of the maneuver—unity with the Socialist Party and the Social Democratic Federation. No, there is nothing there for us. Let the Lovestoneites unite if they wish with the Thomasites and the flag-waving Social Democrats. That is their affair, and we have no objection; they all need a bit of "unity," God knows. But let us attend to our own work—the penetration of the workers' mass movement.

I repeat, if we have not been about this business it is not from lack of conviction as to its necessity. It is simply that we hesitate—or don't know how—to begin in earnest. We have more faith than works, and faith without works is dead.

What We Still Lack

The situation within the radical labor movement has been long since ripe for a decisive turn to mass work, and the objective circumstances are becoming increasingly favorable. What is lacking, primarily, is the necessary psychological readjustment and change in methods of work imposed by the new tasks. The expert programmatic critics, propagandists, and internal faction fighters of yesterday—that's what we were and that's what we needed to be in the conditions of the time—have not yet mastered the art of mass agitation and of simple day to day work in the trade unions and other mass organizations. Too many of our comrades, who can debate any question of the program at the drop of the hat, find difficulty in speaking the language of the unschooled worker who is ready for action and willing to learn.

This is not said to disparage those who have mastered the program and the ability to defend it against all opponents, nor to contrast educational work to mass agitation. Far from it. It is a question rather of complementing the one with the other. The problem which presses hard today and will press harder tomorrow is to interpret and expound the program in such a way as to enable wider circles of workers, hitherto unacquainted with Marxist doctrine, to understand it and act upon it. That is an art which we must learn. We must put ourselves to school in the living movement of the workers. To do that we must get into it. In spite of everything the water remains the only place where one can learn to swim.

Learning by Doing

The workers' mass movement is the source of power, and also of compensating inspiration and enthusiasm for those revolutionary militants who intelligently participate in it. We will see it demonstrated once again at the convention—that those comrades who are learning by doing in the mass movement are the least tainted with pessimism and discouragement, that sickness of isolated, helpless, and hopeless people who contemplate life without living it and see the world mirrored by their own weakness.

The convention will do well to listen attentively to those comrades who come fresh from active participation in the recent class battles—the Briggs strike at Detroit, militant actions of the unemployed at Flint, the epic struggle of the seamen on the Pacific Coast, the magnificent campaign for the independent labor ticket in Minneapolis. The invincible power of the laboring masses in action communicates its enthusiasm and its confidence to its participants, and they, in turn, will help to communicate it to the convention of the party and determine its spirit and orientation.

We have every right to confidence in our future, for we alone, out of a fifteen-year period of unprecedented defeat and disintegration have fought a way forward. Beginning with nothing but a revolutionary program and a handful of people, we have become a movement, if as yet but a small one, and have swept all rivals from the field. Our party is the sole organization of the revolutionary vanguard. Our programmatic disputes with the futile sectarians of the right as well as the pseudo-left—unavoidable in the struggle to clarify the doctrine of the movement and sift out the basic cadres, although they cost us precious years of time and effort—are finished and done. They are things of yesterday and we shall not return to them. Nothing is more foolish than to chase a street car after it has been caught.

The Road is Pointed

Our road now points directly to the mass movement and to the recruiting of hundreds and thousands where once we counted our new adherents in ones and twos. If we have been suffering a certain stagnation, which we do not conceal from ourselves or others, it is primarily because we have not yet made the necessary readjustment of our work to new times and new conditions. From all indications there is every reason to be confident that the convention will survey the situation realistically and give the signal for a speedier readjustment.

I have not mentioned the struggle against the Stalinist party as one of the tasks that are behind us or one that can be separated from effective work in the broad workers' mass movement. Indeed, it is precisely in the trade unions that our militants encounter the Stalinist machine as the greatest obstacle and the greatest enemy. Profoundly wrong are those comrades who, in their commendable zeal to concentrate all activity on trade union work, try to jump over the Stalinist obstacle and [oppose] "constructive work" to the unrelenting frontal attack against the party directed by degenerate turncoats. The party must be clear on this. Otherwise it will not succeed in the mass movement. I will take up this question in my next article.

IV. ON MASS WORK AND ITS RELATION TO THE STRUGGLE AGAINST STALINISM

June 23, 1939

Since the death of Lenin and the beginning of the decline and degeneration of the Russian revolution, the most important and decisive factor in the defeats of the working class has been the Stalinized Comintern. An understanding of this central question has been and remains the key to fruitful revolutionary work. At all stages of the struggle to reassemble the scattered and disoriented elements of the proletarian vanguard, the analysis of Stalinism occupied first place. Those who misunderstood this misunderstood everything and condemned themselves to futility and defeat. Only those who gave the right answer to this question—and the Fourth Internationalists alone did this—were able to move forward and gain strength.

This holds true also for the present and the near future. The center of gravity in all revolutionary work shifts from ideological battles in the isolated circles of the vanguard to mass agitation and the penetration of the workers' mass movement. Here also Stalinism is the most formidable obstacle. Those who ignore this obstacle or deny its existence soon bump their heads against reality. The struggle against Stalinism can in no way be moderated. The forms and methods of the struggle, however, must be adjusted to changed circumstances and new environments. We have yet to do this effectively.

Mass work is a simple enough prescription, but those who try to oversimplify its application have very painful experiences. It is a big error to think good will and hard work alone are enough to gain a leading influence in the mass movement. Parties and groups which operate on such a simple formula usually work for the benefit of others less addicted to Christian ideas.

'Ignoring' the Stalinists

In the past we have heard many lectures on the art of simplified mass work in the Socialist Party, especially from the most stupid wing, the "Clarityites." With a self-assurance born of ignorance and inexperience, they explained how they would win over the masses including the Stalinist workers simply by setting a good example of "constructive work" and "ignoring" the Stalinist party. We know what happened to them, and to others like them. To the extent that they built or helped to build organizations, the disciplined machine of Stalinism took the control away from them and put them to work as errand boys and stooges (Workers Alliance, Auto Union, etc).

No, you cannot ignore the Stalinists. More than that, you cannot gain a single inch of ground and hold it in the trade unions without an intelligent and unrelenting fight against Stalinism. This, to borrow an expression from Grover Cleveland, is a condition, not a theory. Stalinism in the United States has taken on the proportion of a mass movement and has become an evil power of tremendous scope in the trade unions, especially in the more progressive and militant sections. How can any comrade active in the trade union movement conceal this fact from himself? It stares him in the face at every turn. And why should we wish to conceal it? It is necessary to face reality and deal with it. Otherwise we are fumbling in the dark.

Our comrades, with perhaps a few exceptions, understand this very well. Pacifist sentiments toward the Stalinist turncoats and finger men do not infest our movement very seriously. But what we do not yet understand—and we are all more or less culpable on this score, I think—is how to fight Stalinism most effectively in the light of the new developments and under new conditions. Great changes have taken place in recent years in our own position and in the position and the composition of the Stalinist party. It is now generally recognized that the degeneration of the Stalinist party along the lines of social patriotism has become definitive. There is no longer any attempt to conceal it. The pretended revolutionists of yesterday are down on all fours before the imperialist masters. Browder's taste for shoe leather is like a perverted lust. The main concern of the assorted Browders is to convince the masters of the sincerity of their renegacy.

Fighting Stalinism Today

All this has brought about a change in the position of Stalinism and our relation to it. In days past we had to fight Stalinism for influence over the proletarian vanguard. In the main that chapter is closed. The class-conscious revolutionists (naturally ex-revolutionists do not belong in this category) have turned away from Stalinism. The new recruits who constitute the overwhelming majority of the present membership and sympathizing circles of the Communist Party are utter strangers to Marxist doctrine. This transformation imposes not a slackening of our fight but different methods of conducting it.

We began our struggle primarily with programmatic criticism addressed to vanguard workers who knew something about the doctrines and traditions of the revolutionary movement. They were capable of interesting themselves in such questions as "the theory of socialism in one country" and the whole train of theoretical and practical consequences flowing from it. Those who responded to our critical work have constituted the basic cadres of our movement. This was work well done. It was an unavoidable stage in our development, the prerequisite for all that is to follow it. It was in essence a factional struggle within the restricted circle of the vanguard.

Our error consists not in continuing the fight against Stalinism with unabated vigor—that is necessary, more than ever—but in clinging to outmoded methods and types of argument. The average Stalinist worker of the present day finds most of this over his head. What does "socialism in one country" mean to a worker who lacks elementary instruction in the meaning and principles of socialism? What does a deviation from Leninism mean to one who vaguely associates Lenin in his mind with historical figures of bourgeois democracy like Jefferson and Paine? We must find a different, simpler approach to the present-day Stalinist worker. We have to take note of the great differences between him and the Stalinist militant of ten and fifteen years ago and address him accordingly. Above all, we must distinguish between deceived workers in the ranks and the conscious scoundrels of the CP bureaucracy.

A Basic Distinction For Us

The latter point is all-important for our future success. Without realizing it we have been slipping into the same error we once criticized in the Comintern during the frenzy of the "third period" when Social Democratic leaders and workers were all lumped together indiscriminately.

The composition of the Stalinist movement has been profoundly changed. Much of it is worthless, that is sure. The complete adaptation of Stalinism to bourgeois democracy and patriotism has had the effect of attracting toward it a good-sized horde of petty-bourgeois dilettantes and pseudointellectuals who are nothing more than liberals of an especially unattractive variety. But in addition to this trash the CP has acquired a strong following of a different kidney in the trade unions. Discount all the careerists who are bribed by the CP to serve it and all the stupid ones and weaklings who are terrorized, and there still remains a veritable army of militant but unschooled and misguided workers who support the Stalinist party and constitute the backbone of its power in the unions. We will begin to make real advances in the mass movement when we learn how to approach these workers and win them over.

They have not come to the CP, either as members or sympathizers, as a result of a deliberate study of its present program, but in the course of struggle. They have been attracted to Stalinism by a combination of factors—its aggressive methods, its demagogy, the memory of past militancy, the lack of another strong force articulating their sentiments of discontent, etc. They have not in their hearts joined the CP to fight for "democracy." It is not their ambition to maintain the status quo which spells privation and misery for the great bulk of them; but rather, in some way, by collective action to change it. Between these deceived workers and the cynical bureaucracy of Stalinism there is an enormous chasm.

A Deep Contradiction

The contradiction between the leadership and the proletarian sections of the ranks is perhaps deeper in the Stalinist party than in any workers' organization in history. The more openly the bureaucrats announce their apostasy and confirm it in deeds, the deeper must this contradiction grow. The ranks of the CP continually seethe with discontent which is smothered by repressions and expulsions, only to break out afresh. Browder's announcement of a new purge of "spies and wreckers" is eloquent testimony to the internal crisis of the party. This crisis is in its whole essence a reflection of the irreconcilable conflict between the aspirations and desires of the shamefully deceived workers in the ranks and the bureaucrats' cold-blooded and deliberate betrayal of the movement to the imperialist war machine.

Expulsions take place continually. But due, I think, in large part to the ineptness of our work and our lack of a proper approach to the Stalinist workers, too many of them simply fall by the wayside in disillusionment and despair.

We must re-examine the question. We must learn how to appeal to and reason with the former in a friendly and comradely manner and denounce the latter in the tone they deserve as *betrayers of their own membership.*

We must take thought once again of the tactic of the united front. Did it not serve in its day as the best means of separating workers who aspired to struggle for better things from leaders who sabotaged and betrayed that struggle? Why can it not serve again as a revolutionary weapon against the most corrupt and consciously treacherous clique of leaders the history of the labor movement has ever known, the foul bureaucracy of Stalinism?

V. FOR A THREE-A-WEEK APPEAL ON THE ROAD TO A DAILY PAPER

June 27, 1939

A program of expansion such as the party needs at the present time should be a rounded program which sets tasks to be fulfilled in all the most important fields of work. It should aim to push the party forward on all fronts. At the same time, if the program of expansion is not to remain on paper, as the product of irresponsible wish-thinking, it should combine the resolute will of the party to take a step forward with a realistic appraisal of the practical possibilities. Every item of the program should be judged by the convention in this light. We cannot afford to indulge in idle speculation about what we would like to do if we had unlimited resources at our disposal. Rather, our plan, and every separate item of it, must be geared to the resources at our disposal in the shape of human energy and material and technical needs. There is one more proviso, however. In elaborating our plan we must take into account the imperative political necessities of the time, which impose upon us, as a condition for advancement, a greater expenditure of energy, more sacrifices in the spirit of Bolshevism, and a faster pace all along the line.

No Question About Necessity

The proposal for a three-a-week *Appeal,* like all the other items of the program, must be weighed and examined within the framework established by the foregoing considerations. Many factors enter into the discussion of this somewhat ambitious project. Is it politically necessary and advantageous? Have we the technical facilities to produce it? Can we maintain it financially? And finally, can it be effectively distributed by the members of our small organization?

There can be no question about the political necessity and the enormous advantage of a three-a-week publication over the present two-a-week. Things are happening very rapidly in the world today. Problems multiply and questions arise in dizzying succession. A party which answers soonest and oftenest has an inestimable advantage over its slowpoke rivals. The twice-a-week *Appeal,* which has so clearly put us in a commanding position in the radical labor field, is already inadequate for our needs. Here in this issue, for example, we are obliged to print two extra pages to take care of the convention discussion. Apart from that, the editors tell me, their desk drawers are choked with excellent and timely articles and stories for which they have no space; and other vital material, already set up in type, has to be left as holdover on the print-shop stone. The framework of the twice-a-week *Appeal* is already too narrow for our political and agitational needs.

We Have the Forces

Have we the journalistic facilities to produce a paper three times a week without too much difficulty? For one who knows the rich literary resources of our party, to ask that question is to answer it affirmatively. I don't think it is boasting but merely stating obvious facts to say that our staff of writers is second to none, in literary and journalistic competence and political quality. One has only to compare our bright and interestingly written *Appeal* with its dull, gray, and spiritless rivals to satisfy himself on this point. And I refer not merely to the professional staff of the *Appeal,* who are all journalists who know their trade, but also to the occasional contributor, and the small army of voluntary workers and developing apprentices who wait only the call for full-time service.

In addition to that, we have a vast reserve in the shape of worker-correspondents in the field, a reserve which unfortunately has been all too little utilized up til now. Room must be found for the contributions of these worker-correspondents in order to give the paper a more proletarian stamp and make it a truer reflection of the workers' lives.

From a journalistic and technical point of view we could start the three-a-week tomorrow morning without any serious hitch in the schedule.

The Money WILL Be Found

Can we find the money to produce and maintain a three-a-week *Appeal*? This question is not to be airily dismissed. Money, like type, does not stretch; and nobody has yet invented a way of producing three papers as cheaply as two. But on this point our experience with the twice-a-week

Appeal is the best criterion we have to go by. In one sixty-day campaign our comrades contributed close to $3500 to launch this enterprise. Despite difficulties, accidents, and miscalculations, this reserve fund was sufficient to carry us through to the present.

When the convention convenes the twice-a-week *Appeal* will be five months old. With the exception of a crisis a few weeks ago, caused by delinquencies in the payment of bundle orders, we had no serious financial difficulty. Even in that crisis we did not have to appeal for contributions. All we asked was that special efforts be made to pay up bundle order accounts. And the really inspiring response of the branches to this emergency call was sufficient to alleviate the crisis. It demonstrated the determined will of party members to maintain the twice-a-week *Appeal.*

In consultation with the comrades responsible for the financial management of the paper, it has been estimated that we can safely undertake the three-a-week publication if we raise a preliminary fund of $5,000. That can be done not because our comrades have more money than the members of other parties—on the whole they are poorer and have less—but because they have a more serious and determined revolutionary spirit and are willing to pay more for any project which will advance their cause.

Distribution Is the Problem

It is noteworthy that in the comments I have heard and received about the project of the three-a-week *Appeal,* nobody has seriously questioned the capacity of the party to manage it financially. On the financial question, as well as on the technical side, we can speak right now with complete confidence in the feasibility of the enterprise. The convention delegates can be presented with facts and figures on all sides of these two aspects of the question which leave no room for doubt that, from a technical and financial standpoint, the proposal of a three-a-week *Appeal* is no pipe dream but a practical and feasible project.

It will be difficult. It will be a little more of a strain than we were accustomed to in the desultory days of the past. But it can be done.

There remains one more question: Can the three-a-week *Appeal* be adequately distributed by the party members? Here we cannot speak with the same assurance as on the technical and financial sides. The convention delegates who will represent all sections of the country, who have already accumulated a considerable experience with the problem of distributing the twice-a-week, will have to say the word. However, some provisional opinions on this point will not be out of order.

The same question of distribution arose in connection with the project of the twice-a-week *Appeal.* Many comrades who are not at all inclined to pessimism, had misgivings when the twice-a-week *Appeal* was first projected, and even when the decision to launch it was finally taken.

The experience of five months of the twice-a-week *Appeal* has been very illuminating. Despite difficulties, dislocations and maladjustments here and there, the twice-a-week *Appeal,* on the whole, has been effectively distributed. It is a fact that we print and sell twice as many papers per week as we did five months ago. And no more than half of them, roughly speaking, go to the same people. We increased the circle of our literary propaganda by a good fifty percent at one stroke. And those who subscribe to the paper, or buy each issue regularly, get the message of Bolshevism twice a week instead of once.

Humdrum Routine Disappearing

These facts outweigh all other considerations. The publication of the paper twice a week acted as a form of mechanical compulsion upon the branches to devise new and more effective means of distribution. The old humdrum routine had to give way before the deluge of papers coming to the branches twice as fast as before. The system of handing out the weekly bundle order at branch meetings, and perhaps assigning a comrade or two to cover some radical meeting or other, broke down. In order to dispose of the papers the comrades had to get on the street with them. They had to break into new fields. This, in turn, resulted in the establishment of new contacts, and a general invigoration of the life of the party branches. We have seen, in this transformation of the method of distributing our paper, the beginning of a transformation of our methods in general from routine propaganda to mass agitation.

Our party and youth members, by and large, have taken the distribution of the twice-a-week *Appeal* in their stride. There is good reason to believe they will tackle the still more difficult problem of distributing the three-a-week *Appeal* and solve it in action.

If the problem of distributing the paper three times a week looms in the minds of some comrades as an insuperable obstacle, it is pertinent to ask: How and when are we going to distribute a daily paper? We are by no means three-a-week fanatics. We see it only as another transition step on the road to the daily. That is the direction in which we must be pointing all the time. In a country like the United States, above all others, it is somewhat ridiculous to hope to become a serious factor in the political life of a country without a daily paper. It is only when a party ceases merely to contemplate events and to comment on them long afterward, through the columns of a monthly or weekly review, and begins to give answers and to pose actions from day to day, that it breaks out of its propaganda shell and becomes a living political movement.

With the Will to Move Forward

We must aspire toward a daily, and exert every possible ounce of energy to take another step in this direction by the decision of our antiwar convention. The political and agitational advantages of the three-a-week publication do not need to be labored. They are obvious enough on the face of it. The moral effect of the twice-a-week *Appeal* on our members, on sympathizers, on the radical labor movement in general, has already been enormous. A further step forward to a three-a-week *Appeal* will operate similarly, with cumulative force.

A decision by our convention to establish a three-a-week *Appeal*—which everybody will understand is going to be carried out to the letter, for we do not make idle gestures—will ring throughout the progressive labor movement like a clarion and rally new supporters to our movement. It will be felt and said on every side: These Trotskyites stop at no obstacle; they have the determined will to move forward and to conquer. And that's the truth of the matter, too.

VI. ON THE RELATION BETWEEN MASS AGITATION AND TRADE UNION WORK

June 30. 1939

Practically all the serious articles contributed to the party pre-convention discussion by individual comrades, groups, or party committees emphasize the same point: Mass work.

Different proposals are made. There are different evaluations of the past activity of our party. Some comrades offer more ambitious plans, and some betray more impatience than others. But all apparently pursue the same aim, the decisive turn of the party to mass work and the more efficient organization of this work. From this we can see that the party is united at least to this extent: It knows what it wants. So far, so good.

But that does not solve the whole problem. It only poses the problem. The aspiration to direct all attention to the broad masses and to gain a wider influence over them is not new or original with us. There is nothing in this aspiration, of itself, to distinguish us from other parties. Leaving aside the sects and mutual admiration societies, which habituate themselves to isolation as something normal and also desirable, all parties, whether bourgeois or proletarian, strive to win mass support and work out for themselves various techniques of mass appeal.

There Is No Short Cut

An agreement in general on the necessity of a more decisive turn to mass work, such as we appear to have, signifies only that we consider ourselves ready to enter into active and direct competition with all political tendencies for the support of the working masses. Our success in this competition in our time will be determined by how much we understand our own problem and apply that understanding in practice. Here, as our party discussion has disclosed, we run into difficulties and differences of opinion. Some of these differences are simply matters of emphasis. Others represent conflicting conceptions, and that is far more serious. With others, impatience to reach the agreed upon objective is giving rise to ideas which are false in conception and which, if adopted by the party, would have fatal consequences.

One of these false ideas born of impatience is the

idea that we can find a short cut to a mass movement over the head of the trade unions. I mention this first because it is the most fundamental and the most dangerous. There are numerous other misconceptions, all related, however. A considerable section of our movement, in its impatience to get to the masses, is experimenting with ultra-radical nostrums which, ironically enough, are the surest means of assuring a permanent isolation from the masses.

These sentiments are most conspicuous among the youth, whose leaders, apparently, consider it fashionable to play a little bit with adventurism and leftist phrasemongering. If one put his mind to it he couldn't think out a better way of wasting the energy and courage of our young militants and of guaranteeing the eventual reaction of disillusionment and discouragement.

Mass work has many forms. It is necessary to combine them in such a way that each separate division serves the others. The modern proletariat is accustomed to act through its organizations. Most basic and fundamental of these are the trade unions. A party which aims to lead the working class must acquire a strong base of support and a leading influence in the unions. That is what the founding convention of the party a year and a half ago had in mind when it issued the sweeping slogan, "Ninety percent of party work must be directed to the trade unions."

Was this slogan incorrect? Or, has something happened in the past eighteen months to change the nature of workers' organizations and the workers' habit of acting through them? Not at all. But the impatience of some comrades for action is leading them to flirt with the most grotesque ideas in this respect, ideas which they may consider "new," but which in reality are as old as the Marxist struggle against anarchist adventurism.

We hear it said nowadays that the unions are too slow in responding and that we must go direct to the masses. The masses, it seems, are something entirely outside the unions with their seven million or so members. The masses are presumably only waiting to hear from us, and are ready to act without the formality of organization. Even the Ohio-Michigan District Committee of the party, whose jurisdiction covers precisely the heart of the field of the great new unions of workers in the mass production industries, take a rather cross-eyed view of this question. They permit themselves to advocate a program of action which, they say, "can be conducted independently of the limitations and uncertainties of the trade union movement" (*Socialist Appeal*, June 27).

No doubt, the members of the Ohio-Michigan District Committee, who have seen and taken part in workers' demonstrations of power through their unions, knew better. Perhaps they just took a Sunday off for a manifesto spree. Or, possibly, they sought by this high-sounding formula, and the ambiguous verbiage which follows it, to make a "concession" to still more radical comrades who are "tired of waiting for the trade unions." But this sort of concession must determine the correct approach to mass work and firmly reject the false. Otherwise we will have a smash-up.

Deeper into the Unions!

We cannot yield anything from the "90% trade union" formula of the founding convention, not even one percent. Mass agitation in general must be conceived, organized, and developed, not as a substitute for the systematic penetration of the trade unions but as a supplement to it. Woe to the party that despairs of the trade unions and turns away from them! The harder such a party works and the more hysterically it shouts, the sooner it will wear itself out.

Trade union work is not easy. Moreover it is restricted in scope, not complete of itself—herein the syndicalists commit one of their greatest errors—and must be supplemented all the time by the general political and agitational work of the party. But even this general work of the party, unrestricted in its scope by any trade union rules or customs, is directed primarily to the workers organized into unions. They alone are capable of sustained action, precisely because they alone are organized.

True enough, we appeal to all workers; in some cases we appeal most directly and immediately to the unorganized who are the most exploited and deprived. But what is the first suggestion we offer to such workers, if they respond to our appeal? We advise them to join a trade union, or, if unemployed, a union of the unemployed. We cannot go around the unions, and we have no desire to. Our slogan is, "Deeper into the Unions!" Every campaign of general mass agitation must aim to deepen and strengthen our influence in the unions.

No Room for Two Opinions

Trade union work requires patience, endurance, and skill. In very few unions, at present, is it possible to unfold the whole program of the Fourth International. In many unions, dominated by red-baiting bureaucrats, it is necessary for revolutionary militants to refrain from exposing themselves to expulsion by advertising their political affiliations. Revolutionary trade union work, as a rule, in America, is quiet, molelike, unspectacular. To carry on such work unfalteringly; to work in the unions in piecemeal fashion for parts of the program while holding fast to the party, which in its general agitation expounds and defends the program as a whole; to be attentive to the smallest union issues of the day without succumbing to opportunism; to entrench one's self and be in a position to influence the whole union when the time for action comes—these are among the sternest and most important revolutionary tests today.

Such tasks require courage, persistence, and prudence. It is easy to shirk them, or to fail miserably in their performance. We know such cases, and the super-radicalism of the delinquents is poor consolation to the party which needs influence and support in the unions more than it needs anything else. It is easy to fight one's way out of a union by ill-considered tactics, and still easier to talk one's way out. But what the party needs is militants who know how to dig deep into the unions and stay there, gather a circle of sympathizers and supporters about them, and transmute their personal influence into party support in the trade union movement.

The party convention should emphasize this necessity once again. There is no room for two opinions on this question.

FURTHER THOUGHTS ON THE PARTY PRESS

by James P. Cannon

December 21, 1944
(Letter 151 from Sandstone Prison)

The new stage in the development of the party is strikingly expressed both internally and externally. In both fields a transformation of quantity into quality—a veritable revolution—has taken place. It is not the same party that it used to be, either in regard to its internal life and composition or in the nature of its external activity. These changes should be studied attentively from each side as well as in their interrelation. Here I wish only to deal with our external work, with particular reference to the press. . . .

What kind of a paper will best serve the needs of the new party *in the next period* which lies immediately before us? We used to think, or rather take for granted, that as we broke out of the narrow propaganda circle and began to get a hearing from the workers, we should aim at changing the weekly into a daily. That was the motivation for the launching of the twice-a-week experiment and the later proposal, put on the shelf by the outbreak of the internal struggle of 1939, to proceed to a three-a-week issue.

It was also assumed that, as the paper became a "mass" paper, it would be obliged to adapt itself to the political understanding of the average, if not to the lowest common denominator, among its new readers; leaving the more complicated political and theoretical explanations to the monthly magazine. On closer analysis, with the question no longer speculative but concrete and immediate, both these ideas require radical revision.

With our present resources and manpower, and those which can reasonably be counted on in the next period of expansion, a *daily* paper would devour such huge sums as to starve the other departments of our work and defeat our plans for a symmetrical development of the movement. The task of *distributing* a daily would consume so much of the energies of our limited forces as to sacrifice volume of circulation for frequency of issue. The experience with the twice-a-week paper taught us a preliminary lesson in this respect; the circulation *per issue* actually declined despite the added efforts exerted by the party members.

But what we have to *do next* is to reach more and more *new* people, catch their attention at the moment when they are just awakening from political indifference, and try to reach them with our message *regularly.* A big national weekly is ideally suited to this task. And this is a project within our means and potential resources, financial and physical. The whole situation cries out for concentration on the task of developing *The Militant* into an eight-page national paper, published at the cheapest price possible so as to facilitate not merely the expansion but the *multiplication* of its present circulation; a weekly which is not just another radical paper but *the* national paper, dominating the radical labor field.

This is our central task. It is within our means and resources. And its successful execution will help, *not hinder,* the symmetrical development of all other departments of party work—organization, publishing house, and educational system.

RELATED READING

The Teamster Series

FARRELL DOBBS

Four books on the 1930s strikes, organizing drives, and political campaigns that transformed the Teamsters into a militant industrial union movement. Written by the organizer of these battles and leader of the Socialist Workers Party. A tool for workers seeking to use union power and advance the fight for a party of labor. $16 each, series $50. Also in Spanish. *Teamster Rebellion* is also available in French, Farsi, Greek.

The Struggle for a Proletarian Party

JAMES P. CANNON

"The workers of America have power enough to topple the structure of capitalism at home and to lift the whole world with them when they rise," Cannon asserts. On the eve of World War II, a founder of the communist movement in the US and leader of the Communist International in Lenin's time defends the program and party-building norms of Bolshevism. $20. Also in Spanish and Farsi.

In Defense of Marxism

Against the Petty-Bourgeois Opposition in the Socialist Workers Party

LEON TROTSKY

A reply to those in the revolutionary workers movement in the late 1930s who buckled to bourgeois patriotism during Washington's buildup to enter World War II. Trotsky explains why only a party fighting to bring workers into its ranks and leadership can steer a communist course. In the process, he defends the materialist and dialectical foundations of Marxism. $17. Also in Spanish, French, Farsi.

The Communist League of America

Writings and Speeches, 1932–34

JAMES P. CANNON

How the communist movement integrated itself into union battles and social struggles in the early 1930s that signaled the first stirrings of resistance by working people to the social catastrophe of the Great Depression and approaching imperialist war. $25

The Spanish Revolution (1931–39)

LEON TROTSKY

Trotsky recounts a decade of revolutionary struggles and the Stalinist betrayal in Spain that ensured a fascist victory in 1939, making World War II inevitable. $23

The Founding of the Socialist Workers Party

Minutes and Resolutions, 1938–39

JAMES P. CANNON

At founding gatherings of the Socialist Workers Party in 1938–39, revolutionists in the US codified two decades of experience in building a communist party. They charted a working-class course in resisting the coming imperialist war, fighting fascism and Jew-hatred, the struggle for Black rights, forging an alliance with exploited farmers, and the battle to transform the unions into revolutionary instruments of struggle by working people. $23

The Socialist Workers Party in World War II, 1940–43

JAMES P. CANNON

Preparing the communist workers movement in the United States to campaign against wartime censorship, repression, and anti-union assaults. $23

COMMUNIST CONTINUITY AND PROGRAM

New!

Revolution and the Road to Peace in Colombia

The Example of the Cuban Revolution

FIDEL CASTRO

"No crime can be committed in the name of revolution," Fidel Castro declares, drawing from the example set by working people of Cuba as they took state power out of the hands of its capitalist rulers. In 2008, as part of efforts to end six decades of armed conflict in Colombia, he shared the exemplary record of Cuba's revolutionary struggle with the Revolutionary Armed Forces of Colombia (FARC) and the world. $10. Also in Spanish and French.

Lenin's Final Fight

Speeches and Writings, 1922–23

V.I. LENIN

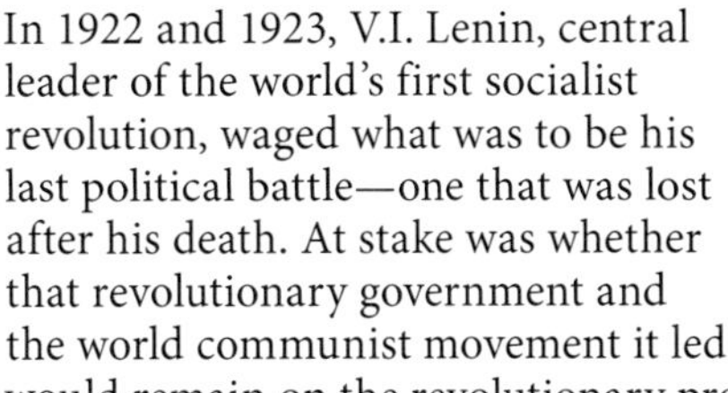

In 1922 and 1923, V.I. Lenin, central leader of the world's first socialist revolution, waged what was to be his last political battle—one that was lost after his death. At stake was whether that revolutionary government and the world communist movement it led would remain on the revolutionary proletarian course that brought workers and peasants to power in Russia in 1917. $17. Also in Spanish, Farsi, Greek.

Their Trotsky and Ours

JACK BARNES

To lead the working class in a successful revolution, a mass proletarian party is needed whose cadres, well beforehand, have absorbed a world communist program, are proletarian in life and work, derive deep satisfaction from doing politics, and have forged a leadership with an acute sense of what to do next. This book is about building such a party. $12. Also in Spanish, French, Farsi.

New Edition!

Cosmetics, Fashion, and the Exploitation of Women

MARY-ALICE WATERS
JOSEPH HANSEN
EVELYN REED

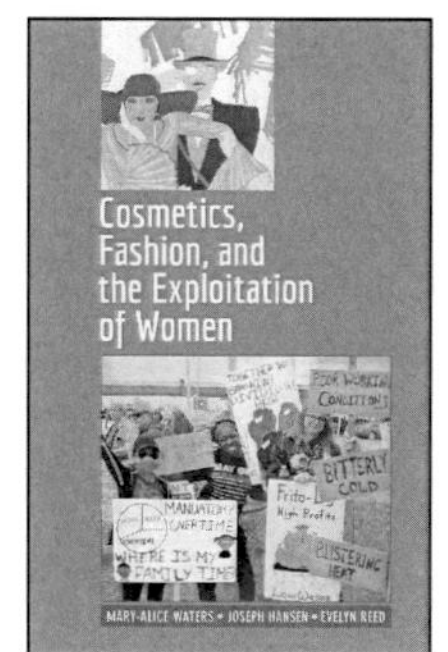

"Norms of beauty and fashion are inseparable from the class struggle." That's the title of the opening chapter of this new edition of a lively 1950s debate in the *Militant*, a socialist newsweekly. How cosmetics and fashion monopolies rake in profits from social insecurities of women and adolescents. Why women's integration into the workforce and unions is a major advance in the fight for emancipation. A Marxist classic on the origins of women's oppression and the working-class road forward. $15. Also in Spanish, French, Farsi, Greek.

Revolutionary Continuity

Marxist Leadership in the U.S.

The Early Years, 1848–1917

Birth of the Communist Movement, 1918–1922

FARRELL DOBBS

"Successive generations of proletarian revolutionists have participated in the movements of the working class and its allies. . . . Marxists today owe them not only homage for their deeds. We also have a duty to learn what they did wrong as well as right so their errors are not repeated." —*Farrell Dobbs*. Two volumes, $17 each.

The Transitional Program for Socialist Revolution

LEON TROTSKY

The Socialist Workers Party program, drafted by Bolshevik leader Trotsky in 1938, still guides communists the world over. The party "uncompromisingly gives battle to all political groupings tied to the apron strings of the bourgeoisie. Its task—the abolition of capitalism's domination. Its aim—socialism. Its method—the proletarian revolution." $17. Also in Farsi.

Essential Works of Lenin

Contains *What Is to Be Done?* as well as *State and Revolution* and *Imperialism: The Highest Stage of Capitalism*. $17

EXPAND YOUR REVOLUTIONARY LIBRARY

New!

Cuba and the Independence War in Guinea-Bissau and Cape Verde

The Fall of the Last Colonial Empire in Africa

VÍCTOR DREKE

In 1974–75 the people of two West African countries, Guinea-Bissau and Cape Verde, put an end to 500 years of Portuguese colonial exploitation. Led by a popular movement forged by Amílcar Cabral, their struggle triggered the collapse of Portugal's entire colonial empire and brought down the 40-year fascist dictatorship in Portugal itself. Víctor Dreke's firsthand account brings to life this decisive victory. $12. Also in Spanish.

Women in Cuba: The Making of a Revolution Within the Revolution

VILMA ESPÍN
ASELA DE LOS SANTOS
YOLANDA FERRER

The integration of women in the ranks and leadership of the Cuban Revolution was intertwined with the proletarian course led by Fidel Castro from the start. This is the story of that revolution and how it transformed the women and men who made it. $17. Also in Spanish, Farsi, Greek.

Opening Guns of World War III: Washington's Assault on Iraq

JACK BARNES

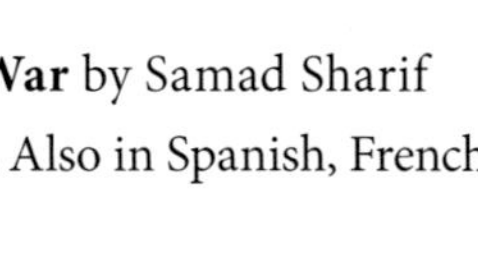

The murderous assault on Iraq in 1990–91 heralded increasingly sharp conflicts among imperialist powers, growing instability of capitalism, and more wars. Also includes:

1945: When US Troops Said 'No!' by Mary-Alice Waters

Lessons from the Iran-Iraq War by Samad Sharif

In *New International* no. 7. $14. Also in Spanish, French, Farsi.

Panama: The Truth About the U.S. Invasion

CINDY JAQUITH, DON ROJAS, FIDEL CASTRO

Washington's probes to retake control of the Panama Canal and broader military operations in the Americas are good reason to recall the invasion of Panama in 1989, at the time the biggest US military action since Vietnam. A threat to the sovereignty of every nation in Latin America, these moves mark US imperialism's determination to crush the example set by Cuba's socialist revolution. Includes speech by Fidel Castro. $5

Labor, Nature, and the Evolution of Humanity

The Long View of History

FREDERICK ENGELS, KARL MARX, GEORGE NOVACK
MARY-ALICE WATERS

Without understanding that social labor, transforming nature, has driven humanity's evolution for millions of years, working people are unable to see beyond the capitalist epoch of class exploitation that warps all human relations, ideas, and values. $12. Also in Spanish and French.

Pathfinder Press **accessible e-books** for the blind, those with low vision, or other challenges reading print books

For a list of current accessible titles, go to: pathfinderpress.com/collections/books-for-the-blind.

Visit bookshare.org for information on how to sign up.